Floral Art

Floral Art

Modern and Abstract Design

BETTY STOCKWELL

Frederick Warne

Published by Frederick Warne (Publishers) Ltd, London 1978
© Frederick Warne & Co Ltd 1978

The author is grateful to Mrs Peggy Moreton for her
help and advice in the preparation of this book.

ISBN 0 7232 2098 0

Filmset by
BAS Printers Limited, Over Wallop, Hampshire
Printed in Great Britain by
Hazell Watson & Viney Ltd, Aylesbury

0023·678

Contents

Man's intellect alone cannot compass
the creation of Art; it must act in
union with the heart and needs
enthusiasm, vision and personal
feeling.

Goethe

Introduction

Today there are thousands of very experienced competent flower arrangers, fully aware of all the mechanics and basic principles of arrangement, providing superb decorations for our churches and cathedrals, our stately homes and public institutions, hospitals and so on, and of course for their own private houses.

These people have a traditional regard for the plant material they use, and however imaginative they may be in seeking new shapes and colours and in creating the unusual and the interesting, they are always mindful of its natural habit of growth.

But flower arrangement when done often in the same places, with a limited range of containers, seems to become a little monotonous. We tend to use the same forms and colour combinations because we know 'they go'. For some of us this is stifling to creativity, and those who do a great deal of arranging or who have to demonstrate and teach arrangement feel there is a need for fresh stimulus to the imagination.

We cannot forever be committed to the same styles, ideas and natural representation; change is coming, slowly but inevitably. But there are also some very practical reasons as to why the nature of our flower designing must change. Many of us live with central heating, which is detrimental to the life of flowers. Fewer people have gardens of any size or the time to tend them. Many live in high-rise apartments without gardens at all and depend solely on what can be bought at the florist's. Here the sheer economics of the matter take over. It is now just too expensive to buy quantities of flowers and foliage every week—and the conservationists have made us more careful in what we take from the countryside.

'So where do we go from here?' some people ask. And they are perhaps a little scared of experimenting with what they begin to understand as modern and abstract styles.

A great deal that passes as 'modern' in all forms of art is simply the disordered outpourings of pseudo-artists, grotesque and way-out designs pandering to the desire for change and excitement. The expression of new attitudes should mean building on previous knowledge and past achievements. So the flower arranger in becoming floral artist will build on existing knowledge of design to achieve a new look.

For the purpose of this book a distinction is drawn between 'flower arrangement', i.e. the traditional use of plant material arranged in all its natural beauty, and 'floral art' which uses a minimum of natural material in creative design. It is assumed that readers have already some expertise in flower arrangement.

Floral art is not necessarily superior to traditional design. But it is quite distinct from it. It is doubtful whether it will ever replace conventional design because we shall always try to link our designs to their settings, and if we continue to use stately homes and old churches for exhibitions we shall continue to use traditional styles. New churches, on the other hand, can take modern or abstract arrangements because the setting is right. There is room for both styles. Let us be open minded and appreciate all beauty from wherever it comes.

Note: Numbers in the text in italic type refer to the photographs in the Plates section.

1. From Flower Arranging to Floral Art

We do not have to continue with an unchanging style. Change is with us constantly in every aspect of our living and is bound to affect the style of flower arranging we pursue. We have only to study the styles of flower arranging in other periods of history to see quite clearly the influences on them of the culture and characteristics of the time. In fact it is an excellent thing to study as many art-forms as possible in the history of both our own and other cultures. This is not difficult today, with the vast resources of public libraries and art galleries and the ease of international travel. All art gives inspiration to every kind of artist.

It is also worth while to try to understand what artists in other media, in our own time, are trying to express as they relate to the world around them.

Variations in artistic style are part of cultural trends affected by social, political, religious, scientific and other developments and pressures. The artist responds to these influences and gradually a new way of seeing arises which becomes common to groups of working artists in many media, and so general style is influenced.

As style changes, people look back and see what they previously appreciated as now old fashioned (as we well know from changing fashion in clothes). But a good design remains a good design despite alterations in fashion: we have only to look at hand-made items of pottery, jewellery or carving thousands of years old to be convinced of this.

Most of us have been familiar with the traditional style of flower arranging for a long time, but are less well acquainted with the thinking behind modern and abstract floral art. The following sections will attempt to clarify the differences.

Traditional Flower Arrangement

Traditional arrangement is characterized by three specific points:

1   All material used appears to radiate from one centre of interest following lines of natural growth.
2   It is usually designed within a pre-determined, three-dimensional shape, often geometric.
3   It has a static though not necessarily symmetrical balance, with the emphasis in the centre of the design.

There are three main groups:

1 Mass arrangements, using a quantity of material in solid shapes (e.g. triangle, circle, oval) with little space in the design, and in fairly large and usually symmetrical containers (*86*).
2 Line arrangements, using a minimum of material to emphasize a particular line, e.g. hogarth curve or S-line, crescent, diagonal, vertical or L-line.
3 Line-mass arrangements, using a medium amount of material in linear form.

Very beautiful effects can be achieved in each of these groupings, working with natural material in as realistic and 'near to nature' way as possible. There is, admittedly, a degree of abstraction in all flower arrangement by the very act of selecting natural material and re-assembling it, particularly in line arrangements; but this is very different from designing in abstract style, as we shall see.

Landscape designs are the most realistic of all forms of flower arrangement. In these, natural material, carefully scaled, is used to suggest a scene—to stimulate the imagination so that, for instance, one 'sees' foreground, middle-ground and distance, or 'enters into' a cave or forest.

Free-form Designs

These have departed from the traditional in two ways. They are not created within a geometric framework, and balance is no longer static. Free of geometric form, they follow the natural rhythms of the plant material. Texture, shape and colour are important. Balance is usually asymmetrical and becomes altogether more dynamic. Free-form has opened the door to far greater creativity over a range of styles.

Contemporary Style

Contemporary style, which is based on the traditional but incorporates ideas of our own times, is usually free-form. It makes use of any and every modern material as the arranger chooses. Its effectiveness lies in the extent to which it unifies the old and the new.

Modern Style

Here we have a distinct break with tradition. The minimum of natural material is used to create the maximum effect. The style is characterized by bold line, form and colour, with emphasis on the use of space. Everything is clean cut and uncluttered, and in consequence has to be most carefully staged. It is less likely to have a radial design and emphasis points are not necessarily central (*42, 11*).

A modern design may use two or more pinholders, containers or vase openings, or have its material positioned on different levels (*2a, 2b, 10*). Parallel verticals may be a feature (*16, 42*). Plant material can be dyed or surface coloured, and manipulated to new shapes. This style is very suitable for ultra-modern homes, but it does not blend with the décor of thirty years ago as well as a more 'contemporary' arrangement would (10).

Abstract Style

The characteristic of this style is that plant material is used for its *design qualities only*, and not in any way that relates to its normal growth habit. A minimum of material is used. It may be cut, twisted, bent, tied, wired, coloured and used in any unconventional way (18, 22, 83). We need to beware that it does not become a clever (or not so clever) form of assemblage, or display art, neither understood nor understandable.

Abstract style falls into two categories: expressive abstract, when the artist seeks to use the elements of the design to express a feeling, mood or idea; and decorative abstract when the artist seeks only to make pattern for its own sake (3, 7a, 7b, 22). These categories will be examined further in the next chapter.

It has been said that the great artist is the simplifier, which gives the abstract artist his justification. To create extreme simplicity requires skill, concentration and considerable thought. All superfluous elements must be omitted and only those parts that really contribute to the idea or design should be included. As one becomes more practised in abstract work and more appreciative of it one can find that a tasteful traditional mass arrangement seems almost flamboyant.

2. The Nature of Abstract Style

When we cease to use plant material in its natural way and use it simply as line, shape, colour, texture, we enter a creative realm where design predominates to the exclusion of all else. When in abstract designing we select a branch, we are looking at it for shape and thickness, considering whether it can convey an idea in a particular way at a particular angle, and not because it is an apple branch with just the right curve. In a truly abstract design no plant material is used in the way it grows naturally. If some items do have to be used in this way—flowers in a container, for example, because they must have water and this is the only practical method—then the design falls into the semi-abstract class. To design within the limits of living material and keep it fresh poses technical problems that sometimes force the semi-abstract approach (*14*).

Expressive abstract is interpretive, expressing the essence of an idea, a mood, an experience, an inner meaning, a psychological comment on life. It is meant to communicate (*8, 25, 28*). Often the idea to be expressed has to be exaggerated in order to communicate it. The design starts with an initial concept—the 'something' that has to be communicated. Now, what will express this best, but without symbolism? What setting will convey the feeling? How will the construction be done to convey the message? Of course, not everyone's interpretation will be the same (*9, 15a, 15b, 19, 29*).

Decorative abstract simply uses pattern for the sake of pattern, design for its own sake, relationships of material to create designs in space or with space, with no purpose or meaning other than the effect created (*13, 22*). The design is often angular but it does not have to be. Depth is important and usually the design can be viewed from any angle. The shape of space is very important too, and material is chosen that outlines it skilfully (*18*). Both are interdependent: either the material thrusts up into space or it encloses space in an interesting way. Sometimes it is arranged so that one movement can be seen through another (*7b*).

No one part of the design dominates because interest is distributed throughout. No item used is necessarily more important than any other item. Each is simply contributing its character to the whole design. Each area of the design is effective according to its ability to attract the eye, the patterns and shapes within the design being more important than the outline of the finished creation. We learn to see units in the design as shapes, e.g. an orange as a sphere, a lily as a cone,

12

gladioli flowers as triangles; but at the same time an artist tries to see the living character of the items used, the grace, vigour, strength and sparkle, and uses these qualities where they are desired, though not in a natural way (63).

We try to achieve a design that is simple, with strong contrasts and good design principles. The eye should be able to take in the whole design, the movements and tensions, in one glance, if a real unity has been achieved (33).

In all abstract designing distortion, i.e. bending, twisting, cutting, wiring, colouring and re-assembling, is used legitimately in as much as it really contributes to the design (34), and natural material will predominate (by a greater impact rather than quantity), otherwise there is a real possibility that the work becomes gimmicky or grotesque. All non-plant materials should be used with discretion and then only when essential to the design, particularly in exhibition work. Natural material can be handled unconventionally, e.g. upside down or flocked or clipped—but when non-plant material is used because this is an easier way of finding the right shape or making it do what you want, then we are in danger of going beyond the borders of floral art into display work or assemblage or even modern sculpture. Man-tooled natural materials, such as balsa wood and wood veneer, play a subsidiary role in the same way as non-plant material. In the course of this book the reader will find that very little non-plant material is considered and very little mutilation to plant material suggested. This is the author's personal approach, built on a respect and reverence for living materials, but does not imply that no such experiments should ever be made.

From the point of view of the design the first placement determines all other relationships. A large solid can be placed anywhere but it needs to be balanced by space (58). Depth is essential. As each item of a design is added the balance is altered. A static balance lacks interest; bad balance ruins the design. A design often stops short of complete balance to allow the viewer to contribute something and to give additional interest. This is deliberate planning and not bad technique (16).

Movement is achieved by directional shapes or masses leading the eye, by overlapping planes, curved linear material, colour and textures.

Colour is a very important factor and if it is necessary to the design it is in order to paint or dye the material. Light colours draw the eye up and out, dark colours draw the eye in or down. In expressive abstract it is also used symbolically (see Chapter 6).

Perhaps most noticeable in abstract work is the increasing tendency to open forms (17). Hans Schoffer is quoted as saying that the movement from closed to open forms 'constitutes *the* great event in the history of modern art'. Looking at the open-form sculptures of Henry Moore and the late Barbara Hepworth we begin to realize the oneness between the inside and the outside of the finished form (30). This oneness is evident in all life, and if abstract floral art is not to become entirely empty of emotion we have to find a way of expressing the internal and external unity of the design in harmonious form.

13

3. Towards the Making of a Good Design

There must be thousands of combinations of plant material that stir the imagination daily. In these it is usually the relationships that have appealed to us rather than individual flowers or leaves—relationships of size, textures, colours, in a particular setting, under a particular light.

How often we take some item of plant material that has caught our eye and made us feel we simply have to use it in a design! We try to use it, without success, and wonder what we first saw in it. The more we puzzle over it the more frustrated and indecisive we become. But stop and consider. This item made its impression when we saw it in its natural setting. What was it contrasted against? How did the light fall upon it? Was it the shape or the colour that caught our attention? Having thought back to details such as these we may find that our difficulty in using this special material is that we cannot re-create the circumstances in which it was found. We must therefore approach our problem in some other way.

To design is to place in planned relationship the material in which we are interested. It is an active creating. It requires that we are sensitive to our material, imaginative about using it, and have the courage to work out our ideas. Ideally we should try to visualize the design we would like to achieve before we start: how by controlled careful placement of like and unlike shapes, of lines or implied lines, of colours and/or textures, we shall create interest and movement, emphasis and significance.

A design that starts well, however, can easily get out of control simply by wavering from the first intention. If too much material is to hand the original design is obscured or lost. For many of us the very quantity and variety of natural material available is in itself overwhelming. We have to learn to be selective, to choose between this and that, to know why we have chosen, and then to remain firm! What we select is determined by the requirements of the design, its position, the effect we hope to achieve, the mood we want to convey. By holding one shape or material against another in different positions we may gain just the inspiration we need. View each item from different angles, wet, dry, in different lights; notice the colour, texture and special characteristics. We must learn to see imaginatively, but this takes time and cannot be hurried. By comparing and contrasting we develop a 'seeing eye' and learn to eliminate items that do not harmonize.

14

We have also to be aware of the limitations of our material if we are to create anything worth while. In the first place, unless we are working with dried materials, we are obliged to have some form of water supply for each item and some way of holding it in position. There are innumerable ways of securing plant material in water or water-retaining substances. These devices may be used decoratively or so arranged that they are concealed completely, but they must be part of the design: nothing should be added as an afterthought to cover up the mechanics. Limitations like this, imposed by the material, need not stifle the imagination. Rather they can be a spur to ingenuity. The design may really come to life as we try to use everything to the maximum of its possibilities.

In designing there is no pre-planned compositional structure, no special formula to be observed, no particular set of rules that must be adhered to. A design should have meaning—not necessarily representational meaning but design significance. It should also have balance, rhythm and emphasis, making for interest and vitality. This can only be achieved by considerable experimentation. It is possible to study the techniques of many artists in various fields and find almost as many methods as there are artists. Eventually we must develop a method of our own, born of understanding and experience. We cannot copy. Some have more natural flair than others and may go further, but all of us can at least try to comprehend the factors that go into the making of a good design, and to these basic elements of design we now turn our attention.

4. Point, Line and Plane

The elements of design in floral art are basically those already familiar to traditional flower arrangers, but must be more specifically analysed and, in practice, more consciously considered.

The Dominant: Spot, Dot or Point

Take a plain postcard and a small dot of coloured paper. Place the dot on the card. Push it round and think about it. The dot, spot, point, is the simplest thing possible and only acquires any importance at all in relation to the card on which it is placed. If you put it right in the middle it is static, uninteresting. Pull it just below centre and it seems to be falling. Push it above centre and it appears to be rising. Push it to one side and notice that the nearer it gets to the edge, the more conspicuous it becomes. Put it into a corner and notice that the edges of the card appear to be pinching it. Stare hard at that spot and notice that its directional movement is inward. It is as if it wants to bore through the card.

Now make a larger spot and repeat the first exercise. Then compare the large and the small spots and notice that as you look at them the larger one appears to come forward and the smaller one to recede. Try a differently shaped spot, pointed at one end for example. Compare it with the round spot. Notice that the shaped spot appears to move in the direction of the blunt end, whereas a circular spot seems to stand still.

Arrange several similar spots on the card (say five or seven). Vary their positions. The spacing of the spots will give either a crowded effect or a loose arrangement. The eye follows from one spot to another, jumping the spaces. See how the differences in spacing can make a smooth path for the eye to travel on or a

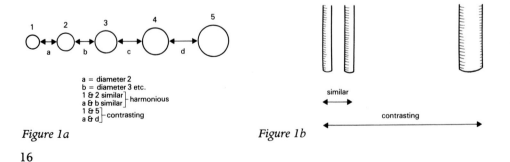

a = diameter 2
b = diameter 3 etc.
1 & 2 similar ⎤
a & b similar ⎦ harmonious
1 & 5 ⎤
a & d ⎦ contrasting

Figure 1a

similar

contrasting

Figure 1b

16

jerky or confused one. Note that the spots appear far apart if the space between them is greater than the diameter of the spots. If the space between them is less than their diameter they then appear to be close together. This is the factor that affects our choice of space interval between the items of plant material selected for any design, including how thick or thin are the stems we select, and the distance we place them apart (Figs 1a, 1b) (8, 19, 20).

Now arrange similar shaped spots in order, from small to large and large to small, and notice how the eye selects its sequences. Grade the spaces between them and note the effect. Mix the sizes and scatter them irregularly and notice how the eye again tries to find sequences or paths to follow and produces imaginary lines between them trying to make them into some orderly formation (Fig 2).

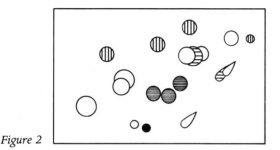

Figure 2

Try overlapping some and see how they seem to try to make holes in the paper! Their very closeness and the overlaps suggest tension and depth. If you can, do this with spots of more than one colour and notice the results. Try one light coloured spot with several dark ones and notice how the light one dominates (Fig 3).

Finally, use shaped spots and place them in such a way that they all appear to be moving.

Perhaps by now you are wondering what this has to do with our subject. But consider what we have found: the spot or dot—in design called POINT—is the smallest, strongest visual symbol in all designing. So great is the visual pull of a point that it can balance a much larger shape. It can also be so overwhelming that it prevents the eye from travelling through a design.

If a point is put far out from the central axis it gains weight and significance and pulls the design towards it. If it is put too low it appears to be falling out of the design. Therefore it can balance or unbalance a design. If the elements in a design are too far apart they remain unrelated and the design has no unity (Fig 4). Adjusting the value or colour of the point to harmonize with another part of the design rather than moving the position may be worth considering.

If short diagonal lines are making a design too exciting or too busy, a point placed to interrupt the diagonals can quieten or stabilize the effect (16). Several

17

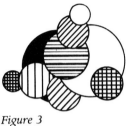

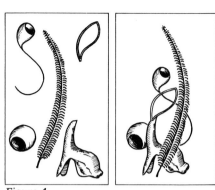

Figure 3

Figure 4

points can create a tensional interest. Several points of equal size, however placed, can overwhelm a design. This may be corrected by turning some sideways or perhaps by grouping a number of them into one visual unit (Fig 5).

It is not necessary always to read 'flower' for 'point', though it often is a flower. The point could be any small, often dark, dominant area. Even a leaf, a two-dimensional area usually interpreted as a plane, can so catch the light, or block it, that it becomes the strong visual point in the design. The point could be a small enclosed space made by the line material used, or even by the crossing of lines.

In her book *Design for Flower Arrangers* Dorothy Riester invites us to take a pencil and paper and draw a leaf (i.e. a plane) with its stem slightly diagonal to the central axis, and then to draw a point in such a way as to balance the plane. By doing this exercise and looking at the examples she gives, one is made aware of the great number of combinations that are possible, simply by varying sizes and stem lengths. Take some leaves and flowers and experiment for yourself.

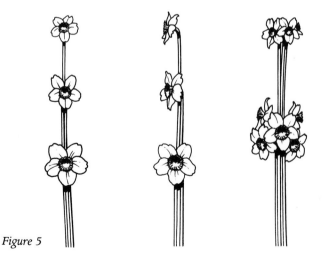

Figure 5

Line

An extension of our exercises with spot, dot or point brings a new element into the picture. One spot attracts attention. Two spots spaced apart cause the eye to run to and fro between them on an imaginary line. The more spots that are added between our first two, the more visible the line becomes.

Line can be a very expressive element in design. One straight line alone has no rhythm and contributes very little to a design. But lines may be bent, curved, spiralled, zigzagged, twisted, jagged, tortuous, suggesting motion and expressing some quality—e.g. quietness, serenity, speed, excitement, restlessness, tension— through the direction of the line and the speed with which the eye can travel along it. Lines can be weak or strong, delicate or bold, stiff or flowing. Vigorous lines present vitality; drooping inactive lines give a wilted look or convey a sentimental mood. The line, more than any other element in design, has a rhythmic living quality.

A line, as we have seen, can be an invisible path between two or more spots. It can also be a directional movement of repetitive shapes, or a directly recorded line as made by a branch or a twig. It can also be the main directional movement of a whole composition and a 'line of continuance' in which the eye is led to and fro, in and through the design (*21*, *26a*, *26b*, *27a*, *27b*). Perhaps this line of continuance is the least easy to see without practice. Try placing a thin piece of tracing paper over a photograph or picture of an arrangement or sculpture or some other work of art, and trace on it the lines of continuance to see how the eye is led in and around the design. It is one thing to do this on a picture and another to do it with a floral design we have created. However, if we hold a piece of exposed blank film in front of our eyes and look at our design we can get much the same effect, probably finding to our mortification that there are no lines of continuance and that we have to twist a leaf, alter a point or change an emphasis to bring the eye back into the design.

The treatment of line in art generally not only expresses the mood of the design but is also related to the mood of the period, to economic, social and cultural developments. Today there are more angular, bent and broken lines, often textured, in all forms of art—in architecture, in poster and fabric design, in furniture and jewellery—whereas some years ago curves and spirals and hogarths (the lazy S-line) abounded. In fact an interesting study can be made of the linear elements in art at different periods.

Association of ideas affects the way in which we tend to see material, and for some lines this has not changed much down the ages. For instance, a vertical line, perhaps because it readily identifies with the human form, suggests growth, elation, support. It is a very strong line, hard, tense, uncompromising. A horizontal line suggests serenity, passivity, peace, calm horizons, rest—perhaps because this is the position we ourselves take for repose.

The point where a vertical line meets a horizontal line is very dominant in

19

any design and usually needs to be counteracted by some alternative area of interest. Visually these two lines appear to advance, whereas a diagonal or oblique line seems to move away even when it is coming towards us (*32a, 32b*).

Diagonal or oblique lines suggest depth in a design by their recessive nature. They are very versatile in that a diagonal line goes through the greater part of 90 degrees either side of a vertical axis and through 360 degrees around the same axis. Diagonal lines can also be used to balance, to slow down a fast-moving line, to counteract a very strong vertical, to create a tensional pull (*40*). As they cross other main lines, or cause a change in direction to a main line, they give a restless, disturbing effect (*31a, 31b*). Used in conjunction with a rather too static line they can give a necessary jerk or sudden movement that will bring the design to life. By themselves diagonal lines are incomplete and insecure, needing an opposite diagonal placement at right angles to steady them (*36*).

Slightly curved lines make for an easy change of direction. They are loose, flexible and give a flowing continuity, suggesting gentle, feminine, soft, lazy ideas. Excessive use of this line results in an aimless weak design. Vigorously curved lines change direction quickly and forcefully and add activity to a design, particularly if they are spiralled (*62*).

Zigzagged and crooked lines are very difficult to use well because of their frequent changes in direction; they need to be contrasted with lines of another type (*3, 28, 35*). Their movement is jerky, staccato, excited, erratic, suggesting lightning, violence, conflict.

Opposing lines, i.e. two or more lines going in opposite directions, usually call for some variation in their thickness. Lines that cross or cause the eye to change direction create tension and give vitality to a design (*13, 20, 76b*).

Related lines, i.e. two or more lines going in the same direction, add emphasis to the movement suggested (*41, 77*).

Compound lines have at least two curves. Several of these in a design will create greater movement than one on its own, but even one will have a strong interest in comparison with, say, a straightforward vertical (*34, 42, 43*).

Plane

The plane is the third basic element with which we work. The dictionary definition is rather obscure for our purposes, but any two-dimensional area enclosed by a line—real or suggested—is a plane. All leaves, from the standpoint of floral art, are planes. All shapes are planes or combinations of planes (*48*). Spray chrysanthemum or golden rod and similar close mass groupings of points combine in one outline to make a plane, in these instances a textured plane.

Take a leaf and view it stem up, stem down, horizontally, diagonally, sideways, back to front, tipped towards the light or away from the light. Does it curve and suggest another shape? At which angle will it contribute most to the design? Really think about the possibilities. Perhaps a leaf of different shape would do your job better? Or perhaps placing it differently is the answer?

A plane can be any shape and it may bend *slightly*. If by bending or twisting or altering the angle of it, it becomes three-dimensional, then two or more planes are made having different directional movements. The surface texture is immaterial, contributing only interest.

Manipulation of planes, tilted for direction of movement, or overlapped to induce a feeling of ascent or descent, helps to give movement and vitality to a design (Figs 6 and 7).

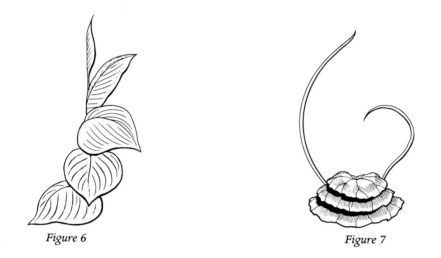

Figure 6   Figure 7

As a plane changes direction there is a corresponding change in the reflection of light. The play of light is an important factor in suggesting depth and interest in the design and will be dealt with more fully later.

Seen sideways on, a plane can become a line, continuing a directional movement already made by other material (*13*). It is important to see the movement of planes within the design. A sequence of parallel planes, particularly if they are almost horizontal, causes the eye to push back into space as in no other way. Any overlapping planes give a spatial illusion suggesting depth (Fig 7).

By training the eye it becomes possible to see areas of colour as planes and this can be helpful in controlling the balance of the design.

5. Shape, Space, Depth and Balance

The term 'shape' (meaning 'form') can be applied to the contour or silhouette of a design. This may be infinitely varied from design to design, but in floral art it is of no great importance in the actual evolving of the work and gives little indication of its structure.

'Shape' as applied to the component parts of a design in floral art refers to areas that are either two-dimensional planes or three-dimensional combinations of planes. They can be open or closed, solids or voids (i.e. spaces) (48), or composite groupings of smaller shapes, e.g. a bunch of grapes. The shape circuit in the accompanying figure (see also the diagram given by Maitland Graves in *The Art of Color and Design*) is a useful aid when seeking contrasting shapes in plant material (Fig 8).

A profitable exercise in assessing three-dimensional shapes is to compare and consider a variety of fruit and vegetable combinations: e.g. apples and potatoes (similar shapes but different textures); walnuts in shell and melons (similar shapes but different sizes); small aubergines and onions (difference in colour); marrow, carrot and pineapple (differences in shape, texture, size and colour).

Figure 8   adjacent shapes: harmonious
opposite shapes: contrasting

Modern still-life pictures often depict geometrical shapes rather than recognizable objects. But most outstandingly strong compositions of all periods are in fact based on some combination of geometric forms, whether circle, ellipse, square, rectangle, triangle or S-shape. It is both interesting and educational to try to discover within famous paintings the geometric shapes created by internal groupings of lines, shapes and spaces. In a design based on a circle the movement radiates symmetrically and the eye is held within the shape. An oval makes for more exciting movement because the eye tends to be directed along the long axis. A triangle with its apex uppermost suggests a movement upwards. A triangle with its apex down directs the eye outward towards each point, which makes for a suggestion of considerable movement. The first three shapes are very much used in traditional flower arrangement. Modern and abstract designs can also use these shapes in outline but their internal design can be totally different in concept.

Space an Essential Element in Design

In designing, the floral artist is concerned with both negative and positive areas, i.e. the selected materials (positive shapes) and the spaces around and between the materials (negative shapes). These areas must be so arranged that the whole composition holds together as one unit (37).

The spaces, or negative shapes, are as important as those areas filled by plant material. In fact, the spaces delineated by your plant material can be more dramatic than the material itself (38).

We know that in a great deal of traditional flower arranging there is so much covering of the mechanics and such a great variety of material used that stuffed space or no space at all is a common result. In floral art, space is a vital part of the composition, an essential element in the design. It is so much an active force in the design that we need to be alert to its importance (4, 30).

A painter of pictures works on a given area with a specific outer edge or frame. He creates his spatial illusions largely by perspective. Floral art is three-dimensional and has no specific frame. As we select our material and place it in position we create height, width and depth. The imaginary line joining these placements, at their tips, makes an outer frame, which of course moves as we move our position and viewpoint. The great thing is to set these first placements in such a way that the eye is only invited to move in and around the design bounded by our material. This movement can be exciting or restful, depending on our use of space.

Space intervals speed up or slow down eye movement: the closer together the spacing the slower the eye movement will be. If you have a fast-moving line in one area of the design, visual balance may be created by introducing close-set areas of tension in another part (39, 44). Alternatively a heavy solid in one part of the design may be balanced by well-spaced elements elsewhere. Visual balance ensures interest throughout the design, not centred in one area.

23

Using size relationships, space becomes a contribution to many interpretive ideas; in all styles of flower arranging it allows us to make a variation of landscape designs. In floral art its interpretive value is usually—not always—more implied than specific.

As soon as we introduce a crossing line into our design we introduce tension (*44*). At the point where the lines cross, the smaller spaces enclosed exert a strong visual attraction. Notice how this visual pull varies as you move a bent stem or leaf up and down, further out, further in, while creating a design (Fig 9). A small enclosed space momentarily holds the eye and creates a pause point, and it can upset the balance of a design if care is not taken to counterbalance it with a larger enclosed space (*14*, *15a*, *15b*, *45*).

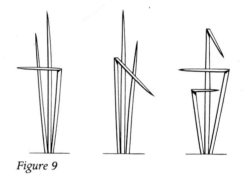

Figure 9

Often a branch or twig may need pruning before it is used in a design; we may need to remove a crossed line or a too-long twig which if left will suggest an enclosed space and upset the balance of our design. On the other hand that may be the very factor that gives life to the design. Check that each piece of material added makes a good space relationship with the other component parts.

The creation of an illusion of space has always been practised by experienced flower arrangers in mass arrangements. They group dark material and place it next to light material and thereby suggest space and increased dimensions of depth. We need to carry this over into our modern approach, using not only dark and light to give depth, but also 'close up' and 'further away' combinations (*46, 47*).

How to Give Depth to a Design

Depth is often more illusory than real in three-dimensional work, unless it is some massive sculpture. In floral art the form has to be considered from front to back as well as from side to side and top to bottom. Therefore each design must have depth and this can be created by the following methods:

Placement—the main lines of the design suggesting a volumetric shape, inviting the eye in and around the design; the container and/or base placed at an angle. Careful spacing of plant material from front to back.

24

Overlapping planes—e.g. individual leaves set almost behind each other to take the eye back into space (Fig 7) (*52*).

Tonal gradations—material moves from light to dark, or dark to light, usually maintaining the same hue.

Colour—an advancing colour used against a receding colour, e.g. red against green; orange against blue; white against black.

Turning of planes—i.e. almost sideways on to a front viewpoint (Fig 6).

Use of light and shadow—allowing for light to fall from one side, or suggesting that this is the case (*25, 64*).

Suggestions of transparency—i.e. that we can see through one plane to view the one behind; similarly that we can see through an enclosed space to the point of interest beyond (*20, 53*).

Planned voids—many flower arrangers know the problem of the hole they try to fill, and filling it create another until the design is solid and lacks lightness or sparkle. In floral art we deliberately plan the hole, or space, into the design as a component, sometimes using a raised base to increase the suggestion of depth below the design (*78*).

Careful use of diagonals and converging lines, together with light and shadow, suggest spatial movements that give depth: concavities or recessions pull the eye in, and convexities or projections pull the eye out. (This effect can be created by the use of colour as well as by the use of design materials.)

The Achievement of Balance

Balance is a subtle thing that relates to our own vertical position and the floor on which we stand. The author well remembers the unnerving experience of walking through a 'trick' log cabin in Mainton Springs, Colorado, where the floor and all the normally horizontal lines such as dado and skirting were at various diagonals, and perspective was so upset that one felt unbalanced and almost compelled to fall over.

The balance of a design also relates to one's own vertical stance and to the visual weight on the horizontal axis. Symmetrical and asymmetrical balance and balance by placement are well understood by experienced flower arrangers. In modern floral art we need especially to bear in mind the important role which the use of space plays in the achievement of balance. We can deliberately place shapes out of balance in order to develop a movement through the design while allowing the space factor to balance the material.

In traditional flower arrangement many designs call for a formal balance (similar visual weights on either side of an imaginary central axis), giving dignified and beautiful results. But most modern and abstract design uses informal balance, or is asymmetrical—the material on either side of the imaginary central axis being totally dissimilar or contrasting (Fig 10). This is less obvious, more dynamic and invites the viewer to enter in imagination into the designing. In informal balance unity in the design must be maintained by dominance (see also 'Dominance' pp. 34–6).

To be interesting a design needs more than one point at which balance is achieved, otherwise it could hardly be said to have movement. We can make use of *contrasts*, dark and light, dull and bright, large and small, diagonals and curves, and so on (and experimentation is the only way in which we learn to use them) (55). Opposing directional 'pulls' can be made to balance by adjusting the angle of the lines or adjusting the size of the planes (40). Sometimes it is a question of cutting or lengthening the stem of a particular flower or leaf. We have already dealt with the 'pull' of a point: balance here may be helped by using a plane in conjunction with the point to adjust the pull. Colour and texture (see next chapter) also add their pulls. A dark area pulls back a light area; a small rough textured area balances a much larger area of smooth texture. We may find that changing a light flower for a darker one, or a smooth leaf for a rough one, may be just what is required to make our design balance (Figs 11a, 11b and 11c) (54).

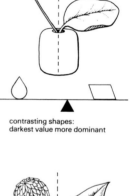

variation of size of shape:
large one dominant

contrasting shapes:
darkest value more dominant

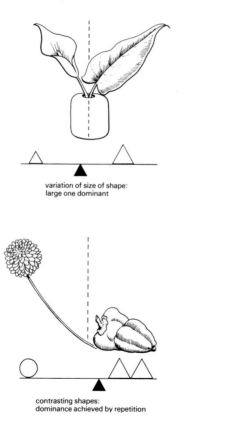

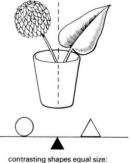

contrasting shapes:
dominance achieved by repetition

contrasting shapes equal size:
no dominance, uninteresting

Figure 10   Aspects of informal balance

26

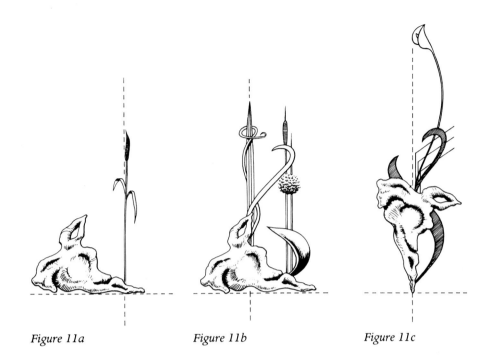

Figure 11a   *Figure 11b*   *Figure 11c*

Visual weight increases:
1   the further the material is from the conjunction of the vertical axis and the
    horizontal axis,
2   the more solid the material,
3   the darker or brighter its colour and
4   the warmer its hue.

Should a design appear squat, a strong vertical line will lift it into space; also
a light or smooth-textured area or a space near the base will tend to lighten and lift
the design.

By careful balancing of the plant material the eye is impelled to move in,
round and through the design, sometimes one aspect seeming dominant,
sometimes another (51, 79). If the first placement of plant material is off-centre
and out of balance, the next placement will automatically be made to restore the
balance. In repeating this imbalance–balance construction as we build our design,
we shall get a variety of dynamic balances that give vitality to the whole. We
should balance not only from side to side but also from rear to front and top to
bottom, using space, directional lines, shape, colour, texture etc. If we attempt to
make a design grow from within outwards we shall achieve a most interesting
effect but this is not always possible or desirable.

27

6. Colour, Value, Texture and Lighting

Who is to judge what makes a good colour scheme—in any sphere? Taste changes with fashion and what pleases one may not please another. Situation, suitability, lighting, personal choice, all play their part.

One cannot lay down arbitrary rules for using colours, because all such rules exist to be broken! If the artist intuitively feels that by using an off-beat, perhaps discordant, combination he has achieved something special or communicated some mood, then who is to say he is wrong?

We all have a natural—even physiological—reaction to colour, and this probably determines our use of it more than education or any particular fashion. Colours, like sounds, have certain vibrations or wave-lengths and, like sounds, can be used in harmonious or discordant combinations. Entirely discordant music is displeasing to the ear, but music with no discords would be dull; similarly, though entirely discordant or conflicting colour schemes are hard to bear in some colour combinations a discordant line can give the vitality and interest needed in the design.

Colour also has an emotional appeal, separate from the form or structure of a design. A beautiful arrangement in colour can look quite ordinary when photographed in black and white. Conversely some arrangements which when photographed in black and white appear interesting, even exciting, can be surprisingly dull when seen in colour.

The emotional impact of colour does of course vary from one person to another, according to their experiences in relation to any particular colour. But to most of us red and orange suggest warmth, fire, excitement. Green suggests the cool fresh peace of herbage; and blue, the cool pure peacefulness of sky. We think of pale and neutral colours as 'quiet' and orange and purple perhaps as 'loud'. Certain colours also have symbolic overtones. Red is often used to symbolize danger and passion; yellow, evil or jealousy; blue, serenity; purple, nobility or wealth; violet, melancholy, negation; green, freshness, youth or envy. Black, white and grey are not pure hues and are classified as neutrals. Among the neutrals white is taken to symbolize purity and truth; grey, old age or humility; black, depression, sorrow or fear.

Incredible as it may seem, it is said that the human eye would be capable of distinguishing about ten million different colours if these could be placed side by side. Yet we mainly confine our working knowledge to the artist's primaries—red, blue, yellow; the secondaries—orange (from red and yellow), violet (red and blue) and green (yellow and blue); and the tertiaries—red–orange, yellow–orange, yellow–green, blue–green, blue–violet and red–violet or purple (1). Shades, tints and tones increase the range. We are also familiar with the complementaries or opposites: red (primary) and green (from the other two primaries); yellow (primary) and violet (from the other two); blue (primary) and orange (from the other two); similarly red–orange and blue–green, yellow–green and red–violet, blue–violet and yellow–orange.

There are various aids to the study and use of colour. The American artist Munsell developed a system now widely used by colourists of all types; the Nickerson fan is in general use with horticulturists, and a colour wheel is published by the National Association of Flower Arrangement Societies.

The Nickerson fan shows a vast range of colours with their shades (addition of black or brown), tones (addition of grey) and tints (addition of white) specified in:

Hue—the pure colour itself
Value—its brightness or luminosity
Chroma—the degree of intensity or purity of a colour

Colour Relationship

We need to bear in mind that colour is relative, and that by adding a touch of one particular colour to a design we may completely change the colour relationship we previously had. Colours affect each other to such an extent that they can balance or unbalance a design. A colour will seem more brilliant and pure against its complementary (e.g. red against green) than against any other colour except grey, which being neutral tends to take on the colour of the complementary. But a deep red will seem almost blue-red against yellow and slightly orangey against blue; if, however, the red is reduced to a tint, pink, the juxtaposition has little effect. Skilfully used, the juxtaposition of colours can create spatial illusion, affecting the size, shape and form of the design elements.

A touch of orange or yellow can make blue really blue. A touch of lime green enhances brownish-gold colours; russet or deep indigo vitalizes green; yellow, gold, copper and brown are vitalized by a touch of blue or black.

A hue may be just yellow or green or blue until it is placed in juxtaposition with a hue tending towards the nearest secondary colour. Thus *Coreopsis verticillata* will look more yellow against an orange marigold and more orange against the pale yellow of an evening primrose, *Oenothera tetragona* 'Riparia'. This is because the eye tends to add the complementary colour of the second flower (i.e. blue to the orange of the marigold) to the yellow of the *Coreopsis* thus making it more green in the first case and (violet to the yellow of the *Oenothera*) making it more red in the second.

29

When a head of orange–red geranium is placed beside some nasturtium of a similar hue but lighter and brighter, its orange–red is dulled. Place the geranium on a rust-coloured dish—a shade of the same hue—and the orange–red is considerably brighter. Place it against laurel leaves and it obtains its maximum brilliance.

Dark tones and colours appear darker when placed next to light tones. The red rose 'Baccarat' is darker in value when placed with light green foliage (e.g. of the primrose, *Primula vulgaris*) and lighter in value with very dark rose foliage.

Value

Value or tonality is important. This refers to the darkness or lightness of any pure hue (57). Everything has value and it is possible to make interesting designs using value without considering colour, but colour cannot be considered without value. Value modifies any pure hue. In fact lit from one side a colour has three values: that of the actual hue, that of the illuminated hue and that of the shaded hue.

White and light-value colours, especially the very brilliant, appear to move upwards and towards you in design; black and darker colours seem to move down and away. Value proportions in a design are very important, i.e. the proportion of light to dark and dark to medium, etc. Almost all designs are stronger for some contrast in values, but one value must be dominant (17).

Colour in Use

As colours have different wavelengths this causes the eye to focus differently. Red has the lowest frequency and longest wavelength and violet has the highest frequency and shortest wavelength. You will notice, for instance, that red imposed on its complementary green at full brilliance gives an uncomfortable flicker or dazzle as the eye tries to adjust to both colours simultaneously. Complementary colours should be used with care. Either one or other should predominate to avoid two conflicting areas of interest in the design. Some complementaries do not look right together if one is reduced to tints and the other to tones or shades, e.g. pale green is not good with dark magenta, nor pale turquoise with dark orange.

We also find that if we reduce a secondary or tertiary colour to a tint—moving clockwise round the colour circle (1)—while maintaining the full hue of the primary colour adjacent (e.g. yellow and pale yellow–green or red and pale salmon) we obtain a circle of displeasing colours. This not only applies to pure colour but also to shades or tones. Sometimes this disharmony is deliberately used in compositions requiring a discordant note, or an acid touch.

Certain colours, e.g. red, red–orange, yellow, belong to the warm side of the colour wheel and are 'advancing' colours. They will always stand out from a background of green or blue and therefore when they are used as a centre of interest in small areas the cooler background colours increase the suggestion of depth. If advancing colours are reduced to tints, the result is usually more attractive and interesting. The more dominant the hue, the less need to create effect.

White, black and grey act as foils for brighter colours, giving a necessary vitality and contrast. To achieve a well-balanced unity, it is desirable to keep the brilliance or debasement of the colours used fairly equally balanced through the design, otherwise certain areas become over-emphasized; therefore one colour or a limited range of colours should dominate the whole. Very pale tints and greyed colours combine easily. The more brilliant the hue, the more careful we must be in using it.

Colour can give an additional rhythmic interest to a design—apart from line and plane and shape. The tension created between colours makes one movement, and the placing of the material makes another. Therefore we need to be careful not to use, for example, just one round red flower as our centre of interest because a red disc is so visually forceful that it would upset all movement in the design. If, however, we can link our red flower with some less emphasized area in the design we can diminish the impact of the red spot and pull the design together. As we create movement with colour and structure, and achieve overlapping patterns, we get a richness in the design.

If any area in a design is already strong because of texture or size or colour it may be wise to link the strong area to one that seems subdued. The converse also holds: a particularly weak area can be strengthened by relating it to a special area of interest or by the introduction of a colour which strongly contrasts with the immediate environment.

Relatively few colours can give the effect of many, provided they are put in the right places. Everything has some colour, if we look carefully enough. It is up to us how we 'play it up'. A dark plane can hold back a light area moving too far forward; small brilliant areas of colour will balance a large area of debased colour.

A good colour scheme pleases the artist, is appropriate for its purpose, has interest and variety, and therefore possesses unity.

Use of Texture in Designing

Texture refers to the 'touch' quality of materials, but by association of visual experience with tactile experience things look, as well as feel, wet, rough, smooth, hard, and so on, depending on how much light a surface absorbs and how much it reflects.

Velvet is rough and absorbs some light; satin is smooth and reflects back most of the light. Teasels are rough, and like velvet absorb some light, but compared with a rudbeckia seed-head which is rough and matt and absorbs all the light, they reflect quite well. Peppers, *Capsicum* spp., are smooth and glossy, bark is rough, laurel leaves reflect, but rose leaves let some of the light through and are matt. In short, plant materials vary greatly in texture. Consider a rose, a sunflower, cockscomb, dock, clematis seed-head, globe artichoke, holly, bark, fungus, *Stachys lanata*, water lily, conker, thistle, peach, gourd, magnolia leaf. Make a collection of as many different plant textures as possible: it is quite an education.

Many things appear rough in texture but are smooth to the touch, e.g. dahlias because of their many petals. The grouping together of several small, smooth items creates a plane of rough texture, e.g. a bunch of grapes or a close arrangement of pebbles.

Very large or strong texture creates 'pattern' as in lace-cap hydrangeas or Michaelmas daisies, where there is considerable space between the 'spots' of texture.

In floral art we use texture as a visual element in designing. A rough texture holds the eye longer than a smooth texture, and for this reason seems to come towards us, whereas a smooth plane seems to recede—an important asset when we wish to create depth. A textured area on the base of the design holds the eye there and could make the design seem heavy. Move it off the base and the eye is drawn up. The further it is moved away from the base the further the eye is drawn up into space. Obviously, the type of container to be used will be as important a textural component as any plant material, sometimes providing the necessary contrast not available in the plant material.

Very great contrast in texture may make a design lack unity and a transitional or connecting item may need to be added. On the other hand, in the many modern and abstract designs which depend greatly on the use of interesting dried material, strong textural interest is very important indeed (*56*).

What we need to be conscious of in our designing is the unity and contrast, the balance and counterbalance, that the use of texture creates (*60*).

Lighting Effects

If the light source can be controlled, as in photography, the effect of varied texture in a design will be much greater, especially if the light comes from a low angle. Shadows emphasize roughness or sharpness in texture; strong light blurs textural variations.

Colour is particularly affected by light and its directional source (*61*). The parts of a design that especially pick up the light become the areas of highest 'value' (*57*). Where the material angles away from the light it takes on various degrees of grey until it is entirely blocked from light and becomes black.

Many people have the experience of doing exhibition work in certain situations where spot-lighting is to be used. The lighting is often fixed after the arrangement is completed, and unless the arranger knows exactly where it is to be fitted and has allowed for it, it frequently happens that the light is so frontal as to entirely flatten the design. Coming from the side, of course, it could greatly enhance it. Light from below, behind, or to one side gives a dynamic spatial effect and creates atmosphere.

Modern design requires that light is carefully planned. Medium light emphasizes texture best. By increasing the light, the value of a colour can be heightened but the textural interest lessened. Smooth surfaces are deceptive: they draw the eye because light reflects from them and can affect the balance of a design. Light can be used to merge dissimilar components into a unity, or angled to make dramatic effects or create moods. It is a medium closely related to colour and by experimenting we discover its possibilities. Do not overlook the dramatic effect of shadows. By these we perceive form (45, 89).

Obviously the onlooker moves in relation to a fixed arrangement and fixed light source, and this fact alone can give life to a rather static arrangement as the light and shade patterns change, modelling and remodelling the form.

Sometimes light is used to create a lively background by putting different coloured gelatins over light sources on either side of a design—by this means a sunset effect could be created, for example. In fact the possibilities of imaginative lighting add a whole new dimension to floral art, but because complicated staging is necessary they are seldom in evidence at exhibitions. Perhaps one day we may see an exhibition in which each design is staged in a light cubicle and the viewers consider the designs from a darkened room—a bit like an aquarium! Quite theatrical effects can be achieved by using fluorescent paint with ultra-violet illumination lighting up only the fluorescent areas. This would also allow changing colours and other possibilities. To be practical, however, most of us must use the light source provided.

A study of light and lighting effects is fundamental to every art. Floral artists lose nothing by devoting time to it. Study how the 'Old Masters' used light in their paintings, and examine its use by modern photographers. Today theatrical effects are created with laser light and most fascinating results are produced by bending light through clear plastic. This could be used in our display stands.

7. Some Principles of Composition

Composition is a confusing term. We are composing as soon as we select one shape or line to go with another. We take a piece of wood, some leaves—different leaves—and perhaps flowers or cones, and hold them together in our hand. We shift them round, remove one or two types of leaf, add another flower and like the result, and perhaps feel we would like to try putting these together in a design. The end result of good designing, of good composition, is the creation of unity within the finished form.

Movement

The effect of a composition is largely determined by the right distribution of accents, or points of emphasis which provide interest, tension or direction, inviting the eye to go from accent to accent, to move through and round and in and out of the design (8). Whether it be through colour, size, texture, directional movements of the material used, the penetration of enclosed spaces or overlapping planes, the eye will seek to find something that completes a relationship or makes a rhythmic movement (62).

A photographer would probably say that a composition gains if there is a 'lead in', i.e. something that leads the eye into the picture. Often this is true for floral art too, but it is wise to avoid pointing a shape or line directly 'out' of a visual 'corner' as this tends to lead the eye out of the design and away from the main interest, even to pull the design apart. Rather, see that the line curves back towards the centre again or that some accessory material acts as a line of continuance and takes the eye back into the design (68). A radiating movement is used less frequently in floral art than in traditional flower arrangement; note that curved or twisted plant material starts with more movement than straight lines.

Dominance or Emphasis

There must be areas of *greater* and *lesser* interest in a design, otherwise the eye is not invited to travel between them. This is achieved by dominance or emphasis and is essential to the life of the design.

If a design holds two or more equal attractions they will pull the design apart. Therefore one part is made dominant and the other subordinate, i.e. one of the competing units must be larger, darker or stronger in colour, or it can have a

34

dominating direction, or it can dominate by repetition (*84*). In some designs there may be more than one subordinate area if the greatest area of interest is sufficiently emphasized. One part, however, must dominate for a fresh, vibrant effect, and to hold the design together. This can only be achieved as the design is executed: emphasis is not something that can be added as an afterthought.

Great care should be taken in the placing of points of emphasis. We need to avoid a 'bull's eye' focal point. A placement of flowers under the tip of the highest point in the bottom third of the design, once normal technique in traditional line design, may, and in fact usually does, make for too static an area in the base of the design, emphasizing the horizontal and preventing vitality. As horizontal emphasis or greyed tones are increased the design becomes restful, sombre or static.

The junction of the vertical line with the horizontal line is already a place of great emphasis. Add the recognizable shape of a figure or creature on the vertical axis and it will command more interest than any other element. Greater freedom of design is expressed by *not* placing a strong accent at the centre or on the central axis either vertically or horizontally, but rather using a light or textured area there to draw the eye up the design into space.

There can be variety in our areas of greater or lesser emphasis; but we have to decide early where the emphasis should be—on line direction, or shape that projects into space, on the size of enclosed space, on tonal values, on repetition, on the interval between elements of the design, or on major contrasts.

Certain colours are heavy, dominant and foundational, others are weak and insignificant. One can use a dominant colour for emphasis, either warm or cool, dominant in one hue, in one intensity, with a touch of its complementary colour to increase the dominance (*67*). A small insignificant area can be emphasized simply by linking it to a colour already dominant in the design; or by introducing a colour which strongly contrasts with the immediate surroundings.

Textured areas stop the eye and invite deeper penetration, but there should be a dominance of either mainly rough or mainly smooth in the design.

A dominant line, probably accompanied by related or opposing lines, usually sets the movement pattern in a design. A major rhythm of curves, perhaps accompanied by a minor rhythm of diagonals, creates lines that the eye must follow (*62, 77*).

The container and the bases used play a very important part in accentuating, or contrasting with, the design. The container is a design element as much as natural material; but take care that a too fussy or too dominant base does not prevent the eye from moving through the design: plant material should predominate over man-made materials (*68*).

In building a good design there must be a feeling of motion and areas of rest, the emphasis points providing these before the eye moves on again. If the emphasis is too strong the eye cannot move on and the design becomes static and lifeless. If on the other hand emphasis is lacking in the design, or if the movement is confused and impossible to follow, the design seems trivial and ineffective (66).

Harmony, Repetition, Contrast and Unity

Harmony is not a requisite of all good design. Harmony lies between the two extremes of monotony and discord. Many modern designs are distinctly discordant and yet have sufficient association of totally unrelated units (e.g. a maximum difference in shape, colour, value, size, etc.) to achieve the unity necessary for a good design (76b). Harmonious elements within a design tend to be similar in shape, size, line, direction, colour, value or texture. Too much harmony can make for monotony rather than interest.

Repetition is usually combined with harmony and contrast (72, 73). Repetition of shape with a variation in size of the components of the design; or repetition of line going in the same direction with a variation in thickness and or length; or a repetition of objects with the same value or texture—any of these variations adds strength to the design (20, 50, 59).

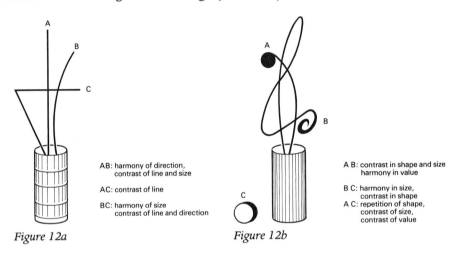

AB: harmony of direction, contrast of line and size

AC: contrast of line

BC: harmony of size contrast of line and direction

Figure 12a

A B: contrast in shape and size harmony in value

B C: harmony in size, contrast in shape

A C: repetition of shape, contrast of size, contrast of value

Figure 12b

Someone said that the true problems of living are always problems of overcoming and reconciling opposites. In composition it is the reconciling of opposites that provides variety within a design. Contrast is essential to a design to give vitality and interest and to create visual tension. It should be used in unequal proportions. Where a unit in a design is made to contrast in one way it may be harmonized in another (Figs 12a, 12b) (11).

The following contrasts are worth considering (Figs 13 and 14):

Contrast of line—curved and straight following the same direction; opposing or crossing following different directions; opposing or crossing, one curved and one straight, following different directions; contrast in thickness.

36

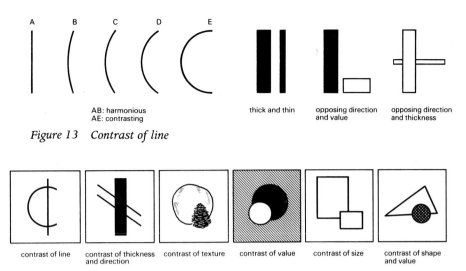

Figure 13   Contrast of line

AB: harmonious
AE: contrasting

thick and thin

opposing direction
and value

opposing direction
and thickness

contrast of line

contrast of thickness
and direction

contrast of texture

contrast of value

contrast of size

contrast of shape
and value

Figure 14   Unity contains contrast

Contrast of size and quantity—large and small shape; small area of strong hue and large amount of dilute hue in complementary colour; small area of white on a light grey background.

Contrast of shape—angles and curves; large space area balanced by small solid area.

Contrast of values/hues and textures—small dark area against a larger light area of different shape, value and hue; strongly textured linear material.

Unity is the end result of good composition (*12, 56*).

As we introduce contrasts we create tensions: by opposing or contrasting lines and directions, between textures, between values, between hues, between sizes and between shapes (*74a, 74b*). This variety may produce interest, but it will certainly also produce conflict unless there is dominance in one part of the design. Where the points of emphasis are placed depends on the design, but there must be one dominant area or major contrast which pulls the design together into a unity (*63*).

Form

Form is the finished design, the completed expression of the idea, the final summing up of the mood, movement, texture and colour, and the various relationships within the design. As you create a design and are sensitive to the various component parts, the space they enclose and the shapes they make, the shadows and the highlights, so you create form (*17, 20, 64*).

Not everybody will appreciate the finished form in the same way. Some people are more developed than others in artistic appreciation, some are themselves highly creative and sensitive, some 'can't see anything in it' and do not want to! We can all educate our appreciation, especially by reading more widely; but though prejudices may give way, preferences remain. Form is something we experience. Whether we appreciate a form or not remains entirely within ourselves. 'Beauty is in the eye of the beholder.'

It is interesting to notice that the contemporary tendency to abstraction in the arts makes for a greater appreciation and understanding of the 'architecture' that constitutes the form. 'Nature has neither kernel nor shell, she is everything at once . . .' (*Goethe*). It is this harmony of 'inside' and 'outside' that gives the finished form its finesse. From every viewpoint the design should be satisfying in unity and interest, having a cohesive simplicity—the sum total of the whole creation being the form.

8. Design Techniques

A New Look at Containers

Containers have a special significance in floral art in that they become very much part of the design and not something to be camouflaged with leaves. The container is chosen for its contribution to the design and is not less important than the plant material.

There are many new and beautiful container designs in glass and pottery. Some have two or more openings or openings on two or three levels, which is very helpful when we remember that radiation of the design elements from one point is not essential to modern and abstract design. In fact, unless the container is so constructed that it does help in this matter it can be difficult to break the habit of years of deliberately arranging the stems so that they do not radiate (this is not to say that they must never radiate, but that they do not have to). In floral art we find ourselves looking at containers in a new way.

Very often there seems to be no suitable container at hand for immediate use. But look around. Usually there are things about the house or readily available that just need working on to make them into excellent containers (*65, 88*).

Invert a large empty fruit-juice tin and cover the outside with a reed mat, or with one of the decorative adhesive fabrics, so that the covering material stands about 4 cm (1½ in) above the upturned base of the tin. On this base a well-pinholder can be concealed (*10*).

Extend a squash bottle with an open-ended can or the cardboard cylinder from a toilet roll. Cover the whole in Polyfilla and then paint (*18*).

A section of drain-pipe and a short section of drain-pipe coupling, both earthenware, can stand together as one container and be painted any colour.

Wire netting, covered with paper or fabric, and then coated with Polyfilla, can be formed into any shape you want, from a dish to a free-form sculpture. By the time it has been painted and/or varnished it will be impossible to tell how it was made. Polyfilla is better than plaster of Paris for this because it takes rather longer to set and allows for adjustments as work proceeds. Plaster of Paris sets hard in minutes. Use exterior Polyfilla if it is to be in contact with water.

Polystyrene can be moulded into almost any shape and painted or flocked (but do not use spray paints without covering in emulsion first). The disadvantage of this very versatile medium is that it is so light. However, if after

39

shaping it is subsequently covered in Polyfilla and a few stones added to the base, a unique and very satisfactory container results (*84*).

Sections of thick bamboo, sections of wire rope, inverted stem glasses, glass bricks, carved Bath stone, string-covered cardboard tubes in various sizes stuck together—all these offer possibilities for original containers.

Plastic containers of all kinds, from bleach bottles to cheese packs, can be converted into something original by cutting off a piece here with a hot knife blade, sticking on a piece there, adding a texture effect with glue and broken eggshell, sawdust, vermiculite or gravel, and then painting (*6a, 71*).

Making Bases

These are most often used to put space under a design, by raising up all or part of it. They can be of clear plastic or glass, or of heavy-looking material such as slate, wood or stone (*25*). Trivets, curved metal scrolls and metal offcuts are useful and rafts made of bamboo strung together are effective (*7b, 71*). Sometimes several types are used together, stems angled out at different levels, or tiered, or in quite a complicated formation of blocks and strips. We have to be careful, however, that the base does not attract too much attention to itself. It must be part of the design and relate in shape to some area of it. And if it can tie in with one or more of the colours, so much the better (*78*).

If a background is used (see below) then the base must relate to both background and design and will probably be of the same material as the background (*81*). Insulation board, cork tile, chipboard, hardboard and straw-board, not to mention plastics, can all be cut into free-form shapes to make the base and become themselves elements in the design (*78*). Space under a base adds lightness to a design. Halved cotton reels make perfect feet.

A base can be used to conceal a well-pinholder. It is possible, for instance, to sink a hole for a pinholder in a felt-covered base of insulation board which is then raised on three short pieces of dowel (*3, 8*). The base can also hide the mechanics for supporting material higher in the design, simply by taking the support through the base. Where a container and a base are covered in the same material they become one unit and the container sinks into oblivion.

Grilles of any sort make good bases. A base in two parts, say two cake boards, one larger than the other, looks more interesting if there is an intervening space. A flowerpot drip tray inverted and put between the board would effect this without showing.

Backgrounds

Most modern and abstract designs are intended to be viewed from all angles, but if the angle of view is to be limited, the background becomes very important because it will be visible through the spaces of the design. A neutral drape is hardly likely to be adequate. The background must be a part of the total design (*76a, 76b*).

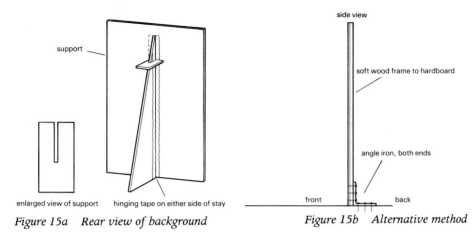

side view

soft wood frame to hardboard

angle iron, both ends

front   back

support

enlarged view of support   hinging tape on either side of stay

Figure 15a   Rear view of background   *Figure 15b   Alternative method*

Backgrounds can be of any shape, irregular, rectangular, oval, three-quarter diamond, or whatever fits best with the planned design. They are usually made of strong card or card mounted on hardboard or plywood. Sometimes hardboard or plywood is used direct—or chipboard or builders' insulation board. Polystyrene, though very versatile, needs support if a large area is used. Any of these materials can be used alone or in combination, closely attached or with spaces between, to increase the suggestion of depth.

Backgrounds stand most securely if made to slot into uprights from a baseboard. Two pairs of plastic expanding cable clips (from an electrical shop) screwed into the back make this a simple matter. Another method would be a prop hinged to the back and a string stay, on the same principle as an easel; or, alternatively, a support, as shown in Figs 15a and 15b. However, there is not always space on the show bench for a back prop and perhaps small feet (as for a fire screen) or screwing directly into the edge of the base would be better. A further possibility is a length of double glazing channel attached to the base to receive the bottom of the background. A central stay may be necessary at the back if the background is very tall. Small, shaped backgrounds can be mounted on projecting battens inserted into slots in the base or into the design mechanics.

Backgrounds can be treated in a number of different ways. They can 'make' the staging, and by painting or texturing can emphasize or complement a design, either in movement or colour, giving another dimension to the concept (*75a, 75b*).

Very often texture is the main contribution of the background and many interesting effects can be achieved. Various types of paper, e.g. crêpe, tissue, metallic foil, wallpaper, veneer, can be used as they are, or cut or torn into pieces and set in different directions so as to give different light angles, or to make ripple movements or suggest perspective. Fabrics offer many possibilities, particularly hessian and felt, dyed towelling and textured synthetics. Muslin can be dipped in Polycell wallpaper paste and crinkled, ruched or moulded whilst wet to give sculptural effects.

41

Collage provides another type of textured background. It can be done with any number of materials: sand, seeds, shells, broken eggshells, string, gravel, rice, tea, sawdust, butter beans, corrugated cardboard, overlapped drinking straws, material-covered card shapes. It can repeat or relate to elements of the design, e.g. in the use of leaves, cypress needles, hogweed, fungus.

Polyfilla while still wet can be combed, pressed or shaped with the fingers. Sculptural effects can also be obtained with papier mâché—which is much lighter to handle and support. PVA glue trailed over a background surface and then wiped over with coloured ink is another method to be explored (82). There is also an enormous range of plastics of varying thickness and colour, and both plastic and fibreglass can be moulded to a limited degree.

Fresh plant material can be used on a background if a small hole is bored at the required level. Behind and below glue a small block of wood. This acts as a shelf for plastic-wrapped Oasis or an extra support for a tube holding water. Both would need additional wiring or taping.

Colour is also important. Black, white and middle grey are usually least interesting as backgrounds, whereas a dark or light grey can be quite effective. If the design is red and green then yellow–green looks good behind. Yellow and purple are neither advancing nor receding colours and therefore are excellent for background.

For other colour effects:

spray one hue lightly over another;

spray colour on chiffon over leaf silhouettes;

use a graded sequence of tones, sprayed vertically;

repeat the contour of the design in a different colour, suggesting a shadow;

two such repetitions could be superimposed and painted to suggest depth;

highlight raised surfaces in light paint with a dry brush;

metallic paper, crumpled and painted with a weak solution of paint, can be rubbed over with a turpentine rag to give a burnished effect;

low side lighting brings out the texture on one side against the colour on the other, but take care that the background does not become predominant.

Just a warning! If you texture and/or colour one side of cardboard or hardboard buckling may occur. So keep the background material taped to a table or similar strong flat surface until absolutely dry—or put counter-battens on the back before starting the job.

Mechanics

Mechanics are a good deal more honest in floral art than in previous styles of flower arranging, but it is most important that they are unobtrusive. The opening of a container is part of the design but the mechanics must be painted or covered just sufficiently to make them attractive enough to be seen. Where pinholders are used they can be covered with polymer chips, glass balls or pieces, lentils etc. It is

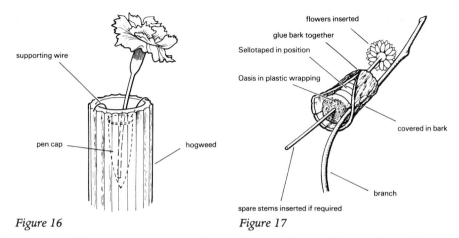

Figure 16   *Figure 17*

best to spread these out on a saucer first and spray them with PVA glue. They then become flexible attached bits instead of 'running' indiscriminately. Sinking the pinholder into the base is another possibility.

Fresh plant material high in the design may have to be supported in water-filled tubes or plastic-wrapped Oasis, either wired or glued to other nearby material or to some extension from the container base (*30*).

Small tubes with attached wires (Aqua-pics) can be obtained from some florists' suppliers. It is possible, though very tricky, to make one's own from Polyglaze, a thick clear plastic sheet sold for cloches and double glazing. If a piece of this is rolled on to itself and touched with a warm iron it makes a neat strong container, flexible enough to support thin stems and strong enough to hold wet Oasis gently pushed in (*18*).

Occasionally it is possible to secure two leaves together to hold a small plastic pocket of Oasis, or perhaps gourds, Chinese lantern or thin bark in the design can be used for this. Alternatively, insert strong galvanized wire into some suitable hollow stems and secure it at the base: the stems can be made to blend attractively into the design and provide a support for the weight of wet plastic-covered Oasis or a water-filled pen cap with the plant material inserted into it (Fig 16).

Flowers that need to be placed individually in some awkward place in the design must not show their source of moisture. Cut the stem close behind the

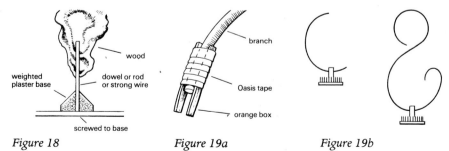

Figure 18   *Figure 19a*   *Figure 19b*

43

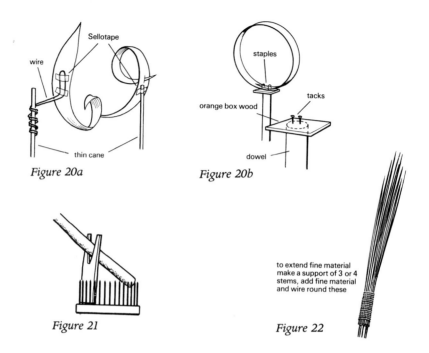

Figure 20a

Figure 20b

Figure 21

to extend fine material
make a support of 3 or 4
stems, add fine material
and wire round these

Figure 22

flower head and push it into a small plug of plastic-covered Oasis. Put the remaining piece of cut stem—or such length as is required—into the other side of the Oasis (its function is purely decorative) (Fig 17) (*81*). Support the Oasis now with the weight of a flower in it, either by taping to a stem, hanging with nylon thread or by the use of a tiny bulldog-clip springhook. Alternatively a short length of plaster bandage can be moistened and moulded into a convenient shape binding the top of a plastic ballpoint pen or similar, holding Oasis, to a branch. It sets in about two minutes and can be painted. Plaster bandages are available at chemists and builders' merchants.

Where heavy items have to be held high, wire or wood supports bedded into Polyfilla may suffice, or maybe a column of Polyfilla, suitably coloured, will do the job. If the whole design has to be lifted, perhaps a dowel screwed to the base would be adequate (Fig 18).

Awkward or very hard stems that will not press on to pinholders and large pieces of bark or groups of dried material can all be wired or glued, at the right angle, to one or more strips cut from the slats of an orange box. This is a soft wood and fixes easily to a pinholder. It can of course be disguised (Figs 19a and 19b).

Today's glues will stick almost anything to anything, but sometimes it helps to use a staple instead, e.g. in the case of leaves curled into circles or rolled back on themselves—and these could again be stapled and/or wired to a thin slat to secure them high in the design (Figs 20a, 20b).

A heavy stem that has to flow sideways may need support underneath, but

44

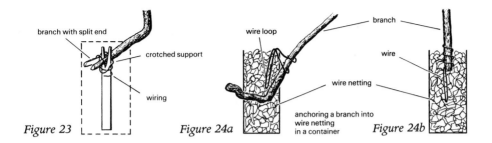

Figure 23   Figure 24a   anchoring a branch into wire netting in a container   Figure 24b

close to the pinholder, to prevent it from falling. A small piece of slat with a V-notch may suffice (Fig 21). Several leaves together (or even one) of fine material will settle more firmly if short lengths of strong spare stalk are wired to their bases (Fig 22). Awkwardly shaped heavy branches, to be used in a tall container, may need a crotched support within the container (Fig 23) or a wire loop outside the container (Figs 24a, 24b).

Sometimes it is convenient to wire or glue several items to one central dowel which goes into the container or on to a base (83). This makes possible a wide angle of flow with a narrow container opening. It is also another method of supporting Oasis.

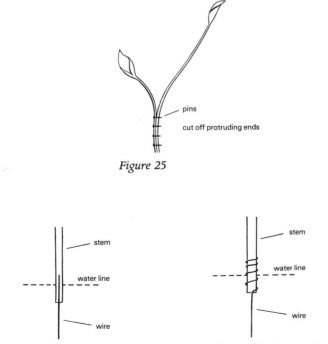

Figure 25

Figure 26   To extend a soft stem

Figure 27   To extend a hard stem

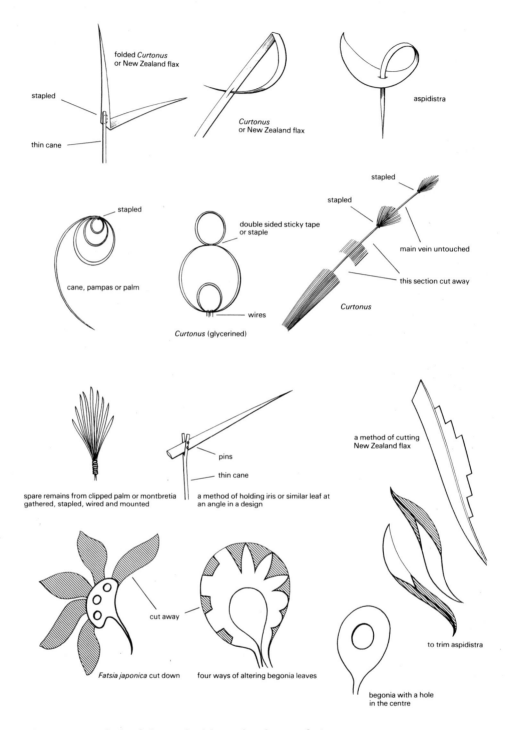

folded *Curtonus*
or New Zealand flax

stapled

thin cane

Curtonus
or New Zealand flax

aspidistra

stapled

cane, pampas or palm

double sided sticky tape
or staple

wires

Curtonus (glycerined)

stapled

stapled

main vein untouched

this section cut away

Curtonus

spare remains from clipped palm or montbretia
gathered, stapled, wired and mounted

pins

thin cane

a method of holding iris or similar leaf at
an angle in a design

a method of cutting
New Zealand flax

cut away

Fatsia japonica cut down

four ways of altering begonia leaves

to trim aspidistra

begonia with a hole
in the centre

Figure 28   Methods of altering leaf forms for abstract designs

46

A few hints:

Stems can be secured to each other with pins and the protruding ends cut off (Fig 25).

Stems can be extended (Figs 26 and 27).

Leaves can be manipulated into other forms (Fig 28).

Cut leaves will shrivel unless sprayed with matt lacquer (obtainable from a photographic shop).

Dried leaves must be steamed or soaked before bending if they are not to split.

Strips of bark can be soaked, rolled round a can to curl, and glued to a cane when dry.

Large bamboo is difficult to position unless placed over three fresh stems 6 cm ($2\frac{1}{2}$ in) long tied together and fixed to a pinholder (Fig 29).

Some plant material, such as sansevieria and succulents, should be kept out of water by pinning or stapling to a narrow batten (Fig 30).

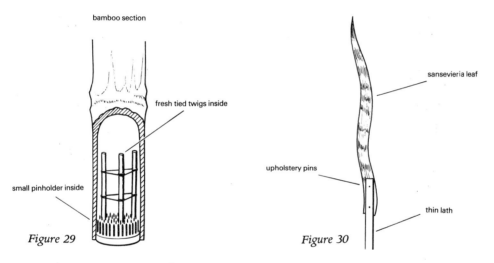

Figure 29

Figure 30

It is very important to be inventive over the mechanics we use, otherwise our modern and abstract designs will tend to be limited to predominantly dried material when we should surely be designing to the absolute limits of our medium.

9. Mobiles, Stamobiles, Stabiles and Constructions

In the realm of floral art mobiles, stamobiles and stabiles are amongst the least seen and least understood. American floral art has staged them for years but in England they still arouse controversy wherever they appear.

Mobiles

Most of us are familiar with mobiles—'units' hanging and moving in space—in every conceivable shape and colour. Those most frequently seen are printed coloured paper designs, ribbon fish or straw stars. Less familiar are fir cones made into little baskets of dried flowers or differently shaped pieces of driftwood. Whatever the items, each is individually revolving, balanced and counter-balanced, making changing patterns as air currents keep the pieces moving.

To make a mobile that is also an effective design is difficult. Ideally the component parts will keep interesting lines and spaces constantly in play. To begin to do this we have to create a support from which the parts may be hung. For exhibition work this would be a frame or stand.

The design might have rings and spheres or varied sizes of geometric or free-form shapes made to interplay from a central placing, or suspended from various positions down a central cord.

A more elaborate method of constructing a mobile starts at the bottom. Select wire of the thinnest grade possible, but strong enough to support your material without bending. Cut a length approximately 20 cm (8 in) and bend the two ends upwards into small loops. From these loops suspend your first two items with almost-invisible nylon thread. (Cotton twists better but is not so strong.) Attach a length of thread near the centre of the wire, adjusting the position to one side until the wire supporting the first two units is balanced horizontally. Secure the thread to the wire with a spot of clear glue, in addition to a knot, to prevent its changing position. The second piece of wire is approximately 25·5 cm (10 in) long, looped at the ends. Suspend your first wire by its central thread to one loop of the second wire, leaving the thread length adjustable. Attach another item to the loop at the other end and then a thread as centrally as possible to again achieve a horizontal balance. This may require an adjustment on the length of the thread supporting the bottom wire. When adjusted, knot and glue into position. Repeat this procedure as many times as desired, each time using a slightly longer wire. It is possible to make two units balance each other on a mobile wider than it is deep. Arrange all the items so that they do not collide. Mobiles, taken to their logical conclusion with controlled settings and movement, become an art form in their own right.

Stamobiles

A stamobile is part static and part mobile. It is fixed at the base and gives the appearance of movement even if it does not constantly move (79). It would be possible for a strong upthrusting part of the design to support a mobile, or more than one if desired (18). The mobile might be simply a suspended *Allium* head or something more elaborate (70). A stamobile could also be a two-part design in which one part is fixed and its complementary part, a mobile, is independently supported from the background. For exhibition purposes such a design would certainly require some type of frame or background to make it a unity.

Nylon thread and various types of swivels and catches to attach prepared units in position are obtainable from shops specializing in fishing tackle.

Stabiles

A stabile, as the name suggests, is a steady, stable, fixed design. It is often portrayed on a very slight base, such as a short length of dowel; sometimes just the tips of the material used act as feet, leaving the majority of the created form in space rather than solidly attached to the base. It depicts movement and vitality within its form but no part of it actually moves (69, 80).

Constructions

A construction is a design fixed with glue, screws, nails, etc, on to a base, forming a more or less permanent structure (9). It can be extremely simple or quite complicated. The finished form and the interplay of the spaces and shapes within it provide continual interest.

Colour and light enhance all these designs.

10. Dried Plant Material

Since dried material lends itself particularly well to modern and abstract design the problems of drying and assembly become particularly relevant. Much has been written on drying but individual experimentation is necessary to discover the most satisfactory methods. It is not always realized that the preparatory treatment *before* drying is the key to good results.

Using a Dessicant Box

Any medium-size grocer's carton that is not too deep will do. The cheapest dessicant is borax, so into this box goes a layer of silver sand (or other washed sand) and borax in the ratio of 2:1. Probably 4 kg (8 lb) sand and 2 kg (4 lb) borax will be sufficient for the first time.

Take a strip of card about the thickness of a postcard, and cut it to the width of the box and 10 cm (4 in) across. Score it firmly down its central length and bend it away from the score mark. At intervals of 8 cm (3 in) cut out V-shaped notches on the central fold. Two or at most three of these strips are sufficient for the box, to serve as rests for the material to be dried. Place supports in position on the layer of mixture.

Many flowers need to be mounted before drying. Using a 20 gauge wire (suitable for most blooms), push a 10 cm (4 in) length into the top of the centre of the flower; bend the trailing end over into a tiny hook and pull gently through so that the hook embeds itself in the centre of the flower. Now gently push each petal up towards the centre of the flower and put a spot of adhesive as near to the base as possible and also against any overlapping petals to keep them in position. Leave to dry about twenty minutes. Treat the required number of flowers before putting in the dessicant box, first making sure the glue is dry on all of them.

Bend the wire in the prepared flower heads a little and rest the calyx of the flower on the notch in the cardboard; the flower is now supported on one side, which prevents the lower petals being squashed. Set the required number of blooms in the box and arrange the dessicant mixture all round, trailing it gently between each petal without disturbing the set of the bloom. Cover the flowers with about 3 cm ($1\frac{1}{4}$ in) of dessicant, seal with foil and leave four to five days.

On uncovering the box check one bloom. If the petals feel crisp to the touch push away the mixture and remove the blooms very gently, so that the full weight of the mixture does not fall on the nearly dry flowers. Finish the treatment by leaving them exposed to the air for 48 hours. This is best done on a cake rack, supported at each end just high enough for the wires to dangle through without putting a dragging weight on the bloom.

Most double flowers dry well by this method: tulips, narcissi, roses, hollyhocks, dahlias, etc. Flowers that have a flat back, e.g. zinnias, can be placed directly on to the dessicant mixture without cardboard supports, shaking the mixture all round and into the petals as before.

Silica gel, also a drying agent, can be used instead of borax. It is more expensive but works more quickly and consequently preserves the colour better. It has to be dried in a cool oven before re-use. For small flowers and smooth leaves there is a finely powdered silica gel and alum mixture obtainable as 'Lasting-Flower' from Lasting Flower Ltd, 6 Wash Lane, Onehouse, Nr. Stowmarket, Suffolk or as 'Cut and Keep' from 2a Rectory Grove, Leigh-on-Sea, Essex. Probably 1 kg (2 lb) and a shoe box will be sufficient for most needs.

Some people use no sand with their dessicant, others substitute cornflour or ground rice, and others use only sand: the method remains the same. Some things dry beautifully, but reds tend to blue and some whites, particularly the waxy ones, tend to go cream or become transparent. Nearly all foliage is successful, retaining a high proportion of green or of autumn colours. There is now a liquid dessicant about to be marketed which presumably will soon be advertised.

Using a Sugar Solution

A strong sugar solution (100 g per litre (2 oz per pint)) or even a weak glycerine solution (one part glycerine to five parts water) will prevent the petals of delphiniums from dropping until they have air dried. There is very little loss of colour but there is some shrinkage of the petals. Clarkia, larkspur and *Spiraea* van Houttei also dry well this way. The very large florets of the Pacific hybrid delphiniums are best treated individually in silica gel if the intention is to use them as separate flowers, otherwise mounting them after drying is almost certain to shatter them. In fact the author has not so far discovered an effective way of using these blooms dry in modern or abstract design.

Pressing

Croton, creepers, maidenhair, raspberry, bracken and many other leaves dry well by pressing and keep their colour for quite a long time. They will of course be quite flat instead of having the curves and twists natural to them. This method is not very useful for flowers unless the intention is to use them for some form of picture collage.

Air Drying

Some flowers, such as *Achillea* (gold plate), will dry with no attention whatsoever.

A large number of small flowers and grasses will dry hung upside down in a dark, dry, airy place. This method is also adequate for most seed-heads. Some leaves, e.g. *Strelitzia*, *Hosta* and *Sycamore*, are very successful when done this way. Pineapple tops hung from three 20 gauge wires pushed into the base dry to make quite eye-catching material.

A little preparation before air drying makes all the difference to the end result. *Allium* heads dry well and make interesting decorative material, but usually they are simply hung upside down and end up with stiff straight stems. However, if a 20 gauge wire is inserted up the stem whilst it is still pliable, it can be manipulated into curves, twists or bends and then left to dry. Many hollow-stemmed flowers can be strengthened and positioned in this way. The wire rusts into them and becomes firmly anchored. Subsequent bending of the wire, however, tends to crack the dried stem.

Glycerining

Use one part glycerine to two parts hot water. It is possible to glycerine almost all foliage with a reasonable skeletal structure. Very soft leaves, e.g. bear's breech (*Acanthus*), *Hydrangea villosa* and tulip leaves, are not successful—though the hydrangea, at least, dries beautifully in silica gel. All foliage treated with glycerine changes colour to some degree, varying from very light biscuit—Mexican orange (*Choisya*) through browns to browny greens and black—unless cochineal, coloured inks or other dyes have also been added to vary this. Some ivy species need total immersion; sweet-chestnut (*Castanca sativa*) needs each leaf treated individually. Some leaves have very weak stems so the main rib and stem must be firmly supported during processing, or rolled sideways on to themselves e.g. *Fatsia*.

As soon as it is apparent that the glycerine is going into the leaves, through the finer veins as well as the main veins, remove from the solution and hang upside down. The glycerine continues down the leaf without being absorbed to excess, which would make the surface sticky. How long to treat depends on the leaves and the colour desired: it can vary from five days to six weeks. As evaporation occurs, top up with water. Two or three small containers of glycerine mixture, filled to about 15 cm (6 in), will be more successful than one large one, when mildew or insect activity can be a nuisance. A light insecticide spray may be useful. If the small containers of glycerine are each stood in a bucket, accidental spills will be avoided.

Some leaves preserve best with a mixture of treatments: e.g. a short spell in silica gel finished by air drying for *Hosta* and *Hydrangea villosa*; a short spell in glycerine finished by air drying for *Veratrum* and *Antholyza*; a short spell in the press, followed by a day in silica gel, followed by air drying for croton, *Codiaeum*.

It is worth knowing that anti-freeze can be substituted for glycerine (at great expense) and that bells of Ireland (*Molucella laevis*), for instance, preserved in turquoise-coloured anti-freeze, becomes a lovely turquoise.

52

Spraying

Some plants and seed-heads and most treated flowers need spraying with clear lacquer before or after drying. Globe artichoke and thistle-type flowers if sprayed lightly before handling will not drop their stamens. As they reach the ripe seed stage they can have all their fluff removed in one hand and be pressed on to a wire-mounted disc of paper covered with a quick-setting glue such as Devcon. Release as soon as firm, fluff out and spray lightly. Clematis and pasque flower (*Anemone pulsatilla*) seed-heads can be glycerined and then sprayed. They will open and fluff out in the glycerine mixture and a spray makes sure they do not shatter. Flowers treated with silica gel have a tendency to re-absorb moisture from the atmosphere and spraying prevents this and delays fading. The best spray to use is obtainable from photographic dealers as a matt, colour-print lacquer.

Skeletonizing

The easiest and most successful method of skeletonizing is by immersion in rainwater. A receptacle of reasonable size should be positioned in an out-of-the-way place and filled with rainwater. Protect this with a lid of some kind to stop mosquitoes breeding and prevent extraneous material falling in. In this, place anything you need skeletonized: leaves (provided they have a strong skeleton, and many have not), seed-heads of Chinese lantern (*Physalis*), Canterbury bell (*Campanula medi*), love-in-a-mist (*Nigella*), and stems of broom (*Cytisus*). Leave for at least two months without disturbing. Remove very carefully on to a tray or some form of support and take to a sink. Wash off the decomposed green, rinse thoroughly and dry on newspaper. Bleach in ordinary household bleach if desired. Some leaves may require a light pressing for 24 hours.

Assembling Dried Material

Flowers The short wires used in the flowers before drying in dessicant will need extending to give height in arrangement. Using florists' tape or gutta-percha tape, start binding just below the calyx. Take a long wire of thicker gauge (e.g. 18 gauge) and place the two wires side by side, overlapping by 5–6 cm (2–2½ in)—do not twist them together—and continue binding over both wires. The tape is waxed and the heat of the hands causes it to stick to itself. The weight of the item to be extended determines the gauge of the wire used. A very heavy head, an artichoke for example, could do with a thick galvanized wire, whilst for a light small flower silver wire might be quite strong enough. For most flowers however a 20 gauge wire is quite satisfactory.

Several light wires can be mounted into one supporting stem to make a spray effect. In this case prepare each item and tape to the end of its individual stem, then take the strong wire or twig that is to support the spray, anchor the end of a new length of tape on this and then add each item without letting go of the tape or breaking it. After wiring the stems into the spray they can be eased into position as desired. Allowance must be made in taping in, for the length of each individual stem and the placement of each bloom or bud.

Leaves   These are mounted by using a short length of silver wire, say 15–22 cm (6–9 in) according to the size of the leaf. The wire is inserted from the front of the leaf, close to the main rib at the bottom, and taken up behind the leaf about one-third of the length. Here it is pushed through to the front, across the main rib and out to the back again and then down to the base, where it is wound three times round the stem and the other end of the wire together. These two thin wires are taped, laid against a stronger covered wire stem and taped to this. According to whether the leaf has to be used singly or as a spray, so taping will continue either to the end of the stem or round other stems on the way down the spray, as for flower sprays.

Occasionally it is necessary to support a leaf with the wire behind it, Sellotaped into position.

Treated leaves are sometimes glued to twigs or inserted in hollow stems (e.g. cow parsley or wheat stems) or glued to other plant material in the design with no special support of their own (*27a, 27b*).

Miscellaneous material   Anyone using much dried material knows that one of the major snags, particularly with imported material, is that it is iron hard and very difficult to fix on to pinholders. Attaching it to a softer wood is the answer. Depending on the nature of the item a short piece of bulrush stem might slip inside a tightly curled stem, or piece of coconut spathe, and stay glued in position (using an impact glue) (*33*). A strip of orange-box slat taped, screwed or glued, or glued and pinned, to the back or side (or even to either side) of a stem may make it manageable (Fig 19a)—and this would certainly be the only way to keep some items like stripped bark in position. Note that before gluing together round stems it is necessary to shave off small portions, making a flat area on both surfaces to effect a good join.

Fungi can be mounted on wire or wood-slat 'legs' (*80*).

In any place where the mechanics would show the fixing may be covered with a mixture of Polyfilla and sawdust in equal quantities, built up in layers to the required amount and coloured to match other items immediately adjacent in the design (*85*). It is not always realized how versatile Polyfilla is. Another use is in supporting difficult stems: strips of material soaked in a Polyfilla mixture and wrapped round such stems will set very hard and make it possible to fix them when they just will not go into position by any other means.

Dried material that has been packed away and become squashed may be refreshed by holding it for a few moments in the steam from a kettle spout and manipulating it into position. But avoid doing this with flowers—they will collapse.

Fresh Plant Material Should Dominate

Although dried material is so useful in floral art we should always try to allow fresh plant material to dominate a design (*12*). This may mean making provision for securing water-retaining substances to our dried material, perhaps by making a pocket between two leaves, or perhaps when taping a join by allowing an extra fold of material to take a cap from a ball point pen to hold Oasis foam (*63*).

11. Using Wood

Wood is one of the most frequently used basic materials in modern design, but many people find it quite difficult to treat and fix properly.

First a Few Do's and Don'ts

DO   remove decayed and rotten wood from your chosen piece, at the time you first find it, where you find it.

DON'T   take rotten wood in the car, or the boot of the car, or home.

DO   remove any obvious creepy-crawlies, and if it has any sign of beetle it is far better to leave it behind than pay to have your loft, garage or furniture treated a few years later.

DO   take a wire brush with you if possible and give the wood a good rub down before taking it home.

DO   leave it outside for a few days for the birds to pick over if you cannot deal with it immediately.

DO   scrub in detergent at the first opportunity and, when dry, wipe over with a cloth or cotton-wool brush soaked in Rentokil if it seems in the least inhabited.

DON'T   store it in a damp place—it sprouts bloom, dust, fungus, etc., and deteriorates.

DON'T   place wood treated with wood preservative below the water-line in an arrangement; the water may reactivate the substance and cause it to kill the flowers.

DON'T   keep heavy pieces of wood and twiggy specimens in the same box. The twiggy bits will get less twiggy each time they come in contact with the heavier bits.

DON'T   try to glue dusty, damp or flaking pieces of wood together. Glue will only secure dry, firm, dust-free surfaces.

DO   be careful to really study the shape of your new-found piece of wood before cutting off and tidying up: although mistakes can be rectified with glue they are never so secure. Before cutting, hold wood at the required angle over the edge of a table, and first mark the exact place where the cut is required.

Methods of Finishing

Bleaching Soak in household bleach in the sink. Roots soaked in bleach will not only be lightened but all grubs and insects will be killed.

Burning Char the stripped wood in a gas flame to acquire a mottled patina; place the wood in the embers of a bonfire and burn it just sufficiently to blacken it. It is sometimes possible to find this ready done after a heath or forest fire (*90*).

Leaving natural Depending on the colour and desired effect, the bark may be the most interesting part. But it will probably peel or split as it ages. If the wood found is already split then the grain of the growth may be the interesting factor. This is best left natural. If the wood is grey, be careful. The grey is only surface deep. If you do have to dig at it and it needs restoring use talc, chalk, or white emulsion paint wiped off.

Stripping As an alternative to sitting down with your knitting and watching TV sit stripping bark from a complicated branch with a sharp knife. It takes ages. Just scrape and peel. Soaking only makes it harder. Coarse sandpaper is too clumsy and, if the wood is soft, scratches it unnecessarily. Green branches, however, soaked in rainwater for six to eight weeks, will shed their bark easily.

Waxing Having stripped a twig or branch, or acquired a nice piece of real driftwood from a river or the sea, wax with a silicone wax to enhance the wood, bring out its natural colour, and help to protect it from wet and dirt. It can be given a surface colouring with shoe polish.

Varnishing This is used on twigs if a 'wet' look is required. For slices of wood that are likely to get water spilled on them, a polyurethane finish is the best. It may be necessary to stain the wood to the desired colour before varnishing. A piece of driftwood, if it is sufficiently interesting, can be given a very formal and sophisticated effect with a little varnish. If the glaze obtained is greater than desired, rub down with a fine sandpaper.

Painting In show work today dyed or painted plant material may be used to heighten the effect of the design, unless otherwise stated in the schedule (*81*). It does remain natural material after all, and when the painting is well done a very modern effect is achieved (*81*).

Sometimes just digging out the rotten wood, brushing with a wire brush, treating with Rentokil and varnishing is sufficient to make an excellent sculpture in its own right (*87*). Perhaps the ideal treatment would be sand-blasting, but few persons have access to this technique.

Methods of Securing

Screwing By far the safest method is to screw the wood to the base with two screws. Paint or stain the top of the base in a lower value and wipe it off. Leave space for a well-pinholder either behind or in front. Make sure the screws are long enough. Countersink them, and cover them and the bottom of the base with felt or baize. This does have the disadvantage of limiting the angle at which the wood can be viewed, and may spoil an otherwise perfectly good base. A screw set centrally on its own lead base can be screwed into the piece of wood to support it; the base being secured with Oasis fix and other material arranged separately (24).

Propping up Use a second piece of wood, possibly glued into position, as a counter-prop. The two pieces can be fixed together with countersunk screws covered with plastic wood, or glued and taped together whilst drying.

Pegging Holes are bored into the main upright and softwood pegs inserted to wedge into position on holder. Again this limits the number of positions for using the wood.

Pinholders Use large, strong, wide-spaced pins. Additional smaller material will need wire or Oasis foam placed over the remaining pins because of the wide spacing. Half and half pinholder/foamholders are now available.

A specially constructed support is now made in the form of an inverted pinholder with an upright adjustable arm, to which the wood is secured. This pinholder fits down on to the pinholder in use. The disadvantage is that the upper pinholder blocks out so many of the pins beneath that it is difficult to position other material close enough to the wood. A similar construction to that just mentioned has a clamp instead of an adjustable arm, but has the same disadvantage.

Fixes Use Permanently Adhesive Clay (PAC) or Oasis fix for lightweight pieces. Plasticine reacts badly to damp, softens in heat, crumbles with age and will not stick to dusty surfaces.

Wire mesh It is sometimes possible to wind wire mesh (sold with fibreglass kits) very firmly round the base of the wood and for some way up its height, thus getting a strong support on the pinholder. This method cannot be used unless there is sufficient material close to the base to cover the wire mesh.

Mounting Wood can be mounted in a base of Polyfilla. The wood will need to be propped up or secured to a base. Made-up Polyfilla mixture is spooned around the base and a well-pinholder pressed into position whilst the mixture is still soft. The pinholder is removed after the indentation is made and the whole allowed to harden. This should stand steadily and can be coloured to resemble bark (85).

Often it is necessary to experiment with a particular piece of wood, and perhaps to use a combination of methods for securing it in your design.

In the event of a heavy stem of wood needing to be at an angle under water, split the stem and insert it into an upright stem. Wire across the junction (Fig 23).

A thick fresh branch can be encouraged to take on a particular shape by partly cutting through where you want the bend to be and inserting a small wedge. If a considerable bend is required it is better to use several small wedges than one large one (Fig 31).

58

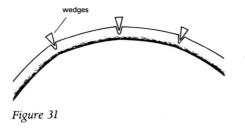

Figure 31

Awkward pieces of looped vine or woody stems that will not anchor easily can sometimes be controlled by attaching slats of wood from an orange-box (from the greengrocer) at the point where the anchor is required (Fig 19b). Being strong and soft this will fit down on to a pinholder or any other mechanics. If the stems still tend to overbalance use a second piece behind, on the other side.

12. Assessing and Judging Floral Art

Assessing Our Own Work

Perhaps we have been inspired and put a design together quickly . . . perhaps we have thought about our work long and carefully. And now that it is finished we wonder whether the result of our effort is worth while.

The following list of points may help us to assess its effectiveness:

1   Does the design continue to give you pleasure each time you see it, or have you stopped seeing it as a whole (as it should be seen) and see only the parts that make up the design? Is it very similar to others that you have done or have you achieved a new emphasis, perhaps using a new container, or overcome a difficult mechanical problem as your design evolved?

2   Take a good look—a really good look. Was it meant to communicate? Does it communicate? Does it really convey the idea you intended to convey, or has this got lost in the making?

3   Does it seem to want something somewhere? Try holding up shapes or lines at different angles in different places and see if this sparks a response. It may suggest what you could do: correct a faulty balance, alter an item, add something more, change a texture or size relationship, change the viewing angle, alter the light source—or perhaps several of these things.

4   By making alterations have you created a new design altogether or really improved your first idea?

5   Has it got lines of continuance? Has it got movement or does it seem static and lifeless? Perhaps the balance is too perfect?

6   Is it an interesting arrangement, not only in the way it is assembled but in the choice of material used? Or is it just a collection of material without real relationship?

7   Does every item in the design work, or could something be removed to make it more exciting, with an opportunity for the viewer to contribute something in imagination?

8   Check the details. Is the base related to the design as a whole? Has the design got depth? Are the points of emphasis well placed, with no one particular centre of interest? Is there one dominant idea? Are the mechanics unobtrusive? Does live plant material predominate? Are the spaces well

designed? Could it be 'cleaned' or would the removal of any item upset or destroy an easy eye-path? Is the colouring imaginative, perhaps daring, or just pretty-pretty?

9   Does the design stand as a unity—are all the component parts fully integrated?

10   Do you have a feeling of satisfaction and achievement because it is all you hoped it would be? Then it probably *is* good!

The Judges' Assessment

Judging ultra-modern designs is difficult enough but judging abstract design is virtually impossible and probably should not be attempted.

Certain aspects can be assessed by the judges. Does the work show excellence of design? Has it originality and distinction? Is there perfection of presentation? If it is expressionistic we can ask 'Does it communicate?' To ask 'Does it conform to the schedule?' presupposes that the schedule has been capable of very wide interpretation; a rigid schedule could be so limiting as to inhibit creativity.

We can appreciate the finer points of design that go to give distinction—the choice of materials and the emotion that controls their use. We can note the rhythmical distribution of interest, the colour and texture, tensions, the timing and spacing, the balance, repetition, special centres of interest, the relationship of the background and all the parts used. But we cannot say that one way is better than another.

Often an arrangement is given a title after the creation of the design. This does not mean that the designer had no particular idea in mind, but simply that the title crystallized the thought behind the design. To be given a specific title to work to might act as a stimulus to the imagination but the finished design should not then be judged as illustration.

Perhaps in future we shall see more exhibition work and fewer competitive classes in the various floral art shows round the country, and such assessment as is made should be purely for keeping the standard high, stimulating new experiments and encouraging greater understanding and appreciation in the layman.

Conclusion

We have seen in the course of this book that floral art does indeed open up new dimensions to flower arrangers. Some of us may not appreciate the new look. It is different. We cannot say that one kind of arranging is better than another, although we may of course understand one kind better, or prefer one to the other. In fact, abstract designing is very difficult to do skilfully and artistically but we are likely to see some outstanding work in this field in the next few years, simply because there are people about with the flair for brilliant design. Already we see more free-form, modern and semi-abstract designs than we did, even a few years ago. Floral art is highly creative and expressive and is rapidly being appreciated on its own merit.

The use of distortion is perhaps one of the obstacles to general acceptance, and distortion in floral art is permissible in the interest of design. Many of us are not yet accustomed to seeing even moderate distortion, but we shall get used to it. Employed with discretion it can convey the feeling of our own times and a sense of the future. But it is a method easily open to abuse and it is our responsibility to avoid this.

There is also a very real danger when any art form is pared down and reduced to a minimum, as in abstract floral art, that it becomes devoid of human experience, unexpressive and without emotion. Let us heed Wordsworth in 'The Tables Turned', Part II of *Poems of Sentiment and Reflection*:

> Sweet is the lore which Nature brings;
>   Our meddling intellect
> Mis-shapes the beauteous forms of things:—
>   We murder to dissect.
>
> Enough of Science and of Art;
>   Close up those barren leaves;
> Come forth, and bring with you a heart
>   That watches and receives.

Bibliography

Many of these books are now out of print but may be obtainable through Public Lending Libraries.

Abstract and not so Abstract Flower Arrangements, Mary G. Knight, Van Nostrand, 1965
Abstract Flower Arrangement, E. H. Cyphers, Hearthside Press, n.d.
The Art of Color and Design, Maitland Graves, McGraw Hill, 1951
The Art of Flower Arranging, Marion Aaronson, Grower Books, 1972
The Art of Flower Arrangement, N. de Kalb Edwards, Thames & Hudson, 1964
Arts and Ideas, W. Fleming, Holt, Rinehart & Winston, 3rd edn, 1968
The Arts and their inter-relations, T. Munro, Liberal Arts Press, 1949
Basic Designs, K. F. Bates, Constable, 1960
Basic Design: the dynamics of visual form, L. M. de Sausmarez, Studio Vista, 1964
A Concise History of Modern Painting, H. Read, Thames & Hudson, 1968
A Concise History of Modern Sculpture, H. Read, Thames & Hudson, 1964
Contemporary Flower Arrangement, Rae L. Goldson, Hearthside Press, n.d.
Creative Flower Arrangement, Jean Taylor, Stanley Paul, 1973
Creativity in Flower Arrangement, Frances Bode, Hearthside Press, n.d.
Design and Depth in Flower Arrangement, E. H. Cyphers, Hearthside Press, n.d.
Design for Flower Arrangers (Revised), D. W. Riester, Van Nostrand, 1972
Design with Plant Material, Marion Aaronson, Grower Books, 1972
The Eye of the Flower Arranger, Lim Bian Yam, Collingbridge, n.d.
Flower Arrangement. Designs for Today, Helen van Pelt Wilson (Ed), Van Nostrand, 1962
Flowers, Space and Motion, Helen van Pelt Wilson, Simon & Schuster, 1971
Form and Space, Eduard Trier, Thames & Hudson, 1962
Forms of Nature and Life, Andreas Feininger, Thames & Hudson, 1966
Modern Abstract Flower Arrangement, E. H. Cyphers, Hearthside Press, n.d.
Nature, Art and Flower Arrangement, E. H. Cyphers, Hearthside Press, n.d.
New Structures in Flower Arrangements, Frances Bode, Hearthside Press, 1968
Order in Space, Keith Critchlow, Thames & Hudson, 1969
The Principles of Art, R. G. Collingwood, Oxford, 1963
Patterns in Space, Richard Slade, Faber, 1969
Search for Form, E. Saarinen, Reinhold, 1948
The Story of Modern Art, S. W. Cheney, Methuen, 1958
The Thinking Eye, Paul Klee, Lund Humphries, 1961

The Plates

1 The colour wheel. The three primary colours—that is, those which are colours in
their own right—are red, yellow and blue. Between one primary colour and another on
the chart are the secondary colours, obtained from the sum of the two primaries. These
secondary colours are orange (red and yellow), green (yellow and blue) and violet (blue
and red). The small circles represent the tertiary and intermediate colours. Opposite
each primary colour is a secondary colour made up from the sum of the other two
primaries. These are the complementary colours. The arrows indicate the three
combinations of complementaries.

2a, 2b Two aspects of the same design. The move to open forms is most noticeable, even using two or more pinholders. Most modern designs can be viewed all round.

3 Interpretive abstract is very difficult to do successfully, since it must not only communicate but also be a good design. This interpretive abstract I have called 'Acropolis' (inspired by a holiday in Greece) and there is a carefully planned balance between the lengths of the pieces of hogweed, between the space intervals and the three placements, and between the related zigzags of iris leaves. The curved dried iris leaves (curved by steaming) contrast strongly with the vertical emphasis and help to increase the visual depth. The zigzag lines are most difficult to use but here give movement and decorative quality to what could otherwise be a rather static design.

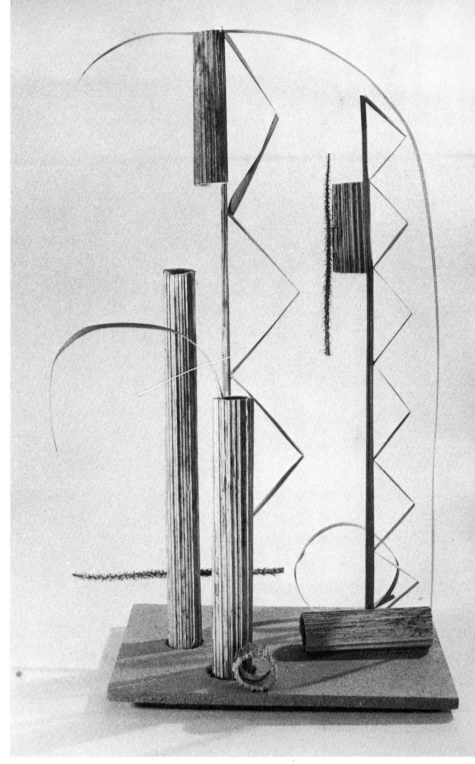

4 This modern design is a good example of the container suggesting the design. Very simple, using glycerined cotoneaster, roses and *Vitis cognitea*, it nevertheless makes an interesting design with a great emphasis on space. (Container by Joyce Withey)

5 Modern designs should not depend entirely on the use of dried material. Here, the lovely long fronds of *Buddleia alternifolia* are used in a new way. The alchemilla leaves relate in shape but contrast in texture, colour and placing. The visual weight of the peonies is balanced by the curve of the container (which was made by Joyce Withey).

6a, 6b These pictures make an interesting comparison. On the right, the home-made container is a bleach bottle, weighted, with string glued into a raised pattern and the whole sprayed mauve. But the leaves are placed with a downward curve effectively stopping the pull of the diagonal movement made by the placing of the peonies. The base makes the design too stable and therefore static. Compare the design below with no base but a second pinholder which allows the horizontally placed alchemilla leaves to make a zigzag eye path, emphasized by the peonies and making the design altogether more vigorous and dynamic.

7a, 7b A decorative abstract design. A student's vertical design depends entirely for its interest on the texture and tonal values within the design. Below I have added a contrasting oblique line, repeated the fungus, giving strength by repetition, and suggested depth by overlapping. The two pieces of *Kniphofia* give a contrast between thick and thin and create a new spatial interest. This then needed a base, made here from three garden canes, cut and strung together. (Student arranger: Mrs J. Deverell)

8   Inspired by the local gas works! An abstract design, using bamboo, hogweed, bent iris leaves and rolled palm leaves. One dried red rose introduces some colour into the beige and brown design. A good illustration of related shapes and space intervals and of interest being distributed through the design. (Bamboo has to be supported by internal stem groups—see 'Mechanics' p. 43)

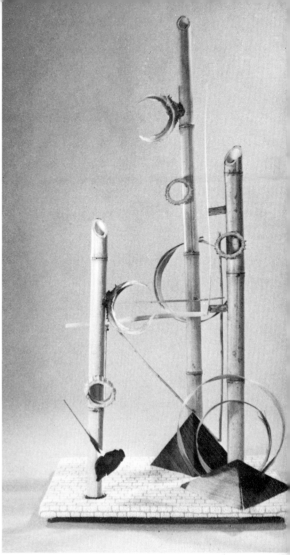

9   Quayside—interpretive abstract, using bent *Kniphofia* stems with wheat stems cut to differing lengths and glued to the main supports. The whole is mounted in Polyfilla.

10　A coffee jar, extended with
a tin and a well-pinholder and
covered in a straw place mat,
makes a harmonious container
for this modern design of
Nitidia root and *Fatsia japonica*
leaves with the yellow
chrysanthemums. A second
well-pinholder supports the
lower material and produces a
maximum effect with a
minimum of material, typical of
so many modern arrangements.

11　Eucalyptus bark, fungus and curved dried iris leaves are the basis of this modern design. The container is a coffee jar covered in Contact. Two well-pinholders are used. Colour is introduced on the base by rolled red velvet, relating to the two carnations, the seed-head relates to the bark and the stalk relates to the dried iris loops. Relating components through colour, value, shape and texture, repetition, etc. is the key to making rhythms within the design.

12　A modern design. Monkey puzzle tree has tremendous textural interest but is heavy and hard and not easy to use. This has been mounted into plaster of Paris with a well-pinholder between the two pieces. Contrasting in texture and shape are the bamboo. In order to relate the roses to the bamboo I have used two curls of wood shavings.

13 A design based entirely on varied planes and the spaces created between them. The pinholder is under the base and the material successfully hides any mechanics. There is a careful contrast between round and triangular shapes and between curved and straight lines.

14 A semi-abstract design. A triangular element in the design may find a repeat in the base or in other triangles at opposing lines. Two iris leaves are bent and pierced through two others to form the triangles. The container is a block of Polyfilla. The placing of the dahlias, one going back and the other coming forward, helps to increase depth. The overlapped triangular dahlia petals forming the shape of the flower make a very strong emphasis.

15a, 15b A good illustration of the difference between a modern design and a semi-abstract design. Both are a reflection on living conditions—**a** living today, and **b** living tomorrow. There are strong tensions in both designs. Notice the differences by comparison.

16 Utterly different from any other design, the vertical driftwood and horizontal seed-husk make a curiously balanced frame, against which the *Surowii statice* has been carefully arranged on the diagonal. Some of the Oasis is taller, behind the wood, to allow the diagonals to remain parallel to each other. Two pieces of *Statice* are bent to run counter to the diagonal movement giving contrast and tensions. The roses run diagonally across the *Statice* towards the back, the back one seen through the *Statice* suggesting transparency. and depth. The curious balance is caused by the graduation of the seed-husk. Place a pencil in this position and see the design stabilize and become static.

17 An abstract emphasis on form, and the play of rhythms within the whole. The containers are two sections of dried *Opuntia* stem and two of the circles within the design are individual leaf stubs lifted from them. Two pieces of eucalyptus bark and a large seed-pod make the main shape, curved skeletonized aspidistra, clipped palm and cane string are the other components. Both flowers have their stems individually wrapped in wet Oasis and polythene and are then inserted, one in the bark, the other attached to a loop of dried seaweed. There is a pleasing proportion of light, dark and medium values.

18 Completely abstract in design, the rather large area on the left incorporates a leaf mobile to balance the stronger area below. The container is a squash bottle and toilet roll interior, covered with Polyfilla. The base is a slice of olive wood. The flowers are inserted into Oasis in polythene, covered in thin eucalyptus bark and secured to the main lengths of Russian vine. The whole has a swinging rhythm through colour, line and shape.

19 Interpretive abstract to suggest the scientist. The balls are flocked polystyrene, one of which is suspended by nylon thread to give the tensional interest necessary to that area of the design. Notice the material is supported by pinholders sunk into the base.

20 In abstract design nothing is used in a natural manner, but a good design is more important than ever. Here hogweed and *Kniphofia* seed-heads and stems have been used with palm husks and one curled skeletonized aspidistra to make a carefully related design. There is a planned relationship between the heights, thicknesses, space intervals, textures and curved and horizontal contrasts and the play of tensions and enclosed spaces. A carefully composed abstract design is as easy to live with as a beautiful traditional flower arrangement in all its flamboyance.

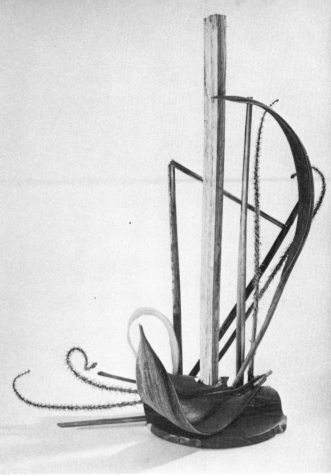

21 A modern design. The points of emphasis give direction and interest, inviting the eye to go from accent to accent through the design, either from the dark shell and up the leaves to the seed-heads or from the lighter shell up the flowers to the space between the seed-heads.

22 Non-objective abstract—design for the sake of design. A hollowed root contains an aerosol lid holding Oasis sec. This supports wild evening primrose seed heads bleached and curled aspidistra (see section on 'Mechanics' p. 42), curled and mounted silver birch bark and one rose in the outside casing of a green felt tip pen, sealed at the bottom and water-filled.

23 A modern design in a large dried fungus. By bending the iris leaves, strong tensional interest and space is created. The circular shape of the *Alchemilla modis* leaf contrasts with the triangles and relates to the flowers and fungus, although contrasting in texture and colour.

24 'Mother and Child'. An abstract design using stripped ivy and a twist of seaweed, both sprayed purple. The child is picked out with a suggestion of fluorescent orange paint, linking the roses and the base.

25 Abstract design can be either decorative or interpretive. This is interpretive and intended to suggest the 'Changing of the Guard'.

Compare photographs **26a** and **26b**.

26a A line of continuance from the slate, up the left of the irregular lines of the modern pottery vase, down and up the *Mahonia* leaf, across the arum lilies to the upper part of the driftwood, to the lower tip, across the shadow and back to the base.

26b The strong movement is the diagonal from the lower tip of the driftwood to the higher arum and it becomes difficult for the eye to pick up the line of continuance through the design.

27a, 27b In this abstract design of aspidistra and *Allium*, notice the importance of the placing of the bottom *Allium* head in these two photographs. On the left it points back into the design so that there is a lower triangle relating to the triangle at the top. It also by transparency suggests depth and the open end of the bamboo container relates rhythmically to the *Allium* heads. On the right the *Allium* is angled out of the design, which stops the eye making a line of continuance and leaves the bottom of the design weak and unrelated. This is a strong vertical design with contrasting oblique lines and sufficient curves to give a dynamic effect.

28 Interpretive Abstract. 'He is not here, He is risen.' An Easter design using ivy screwed to a tree root. The suggestion of a schism through the tomb is made by the blackened diagonals (which also give essential vitality to the design). The angels in the two lilies are supported in a hogweed stem (the two stems being horizontally pinned together and the ends snipped off). A rather sombre design over 94 cm (3 ft) high, with considerable drama.

29 An abstract interpretation of Elstree Reservoir in winter! Set on two pinholders, 20 cm (8 in) apart, covered in bark, with holes through to take the upright placements. Looking from the foreground (looped *Curtonus* and faciated *Forsythia*) we look across the sun-dappled water (palm seed stems) to the bare trees the other side (faciated *Forsythia* and folded *Curtonus*). The chrysanthemum (its stem secured in a ballpoint pen top holding Oasis) represents the sun, the carnation represents its reflection and the fungus the light shimmer. Having a light area in the fungus the eye is lifted up from the rough texture of the bark and swings into the design. Considerable care has been taken to get the space intervals and rhythms within the design. No two people would see this scene the same way or have the same material with which to interpret it.

30 Typical of modern and abstract design, the enclosed form contains within itself the rhythms and interests of the whole. It is not always possible to create a design in which you can see the inner and outer meaning at the same time. The light tracery of the *Polygonum baldschuanicum*, or Russian vine, contrasted with the ornopordon leaves, makes this possible. The top rose is secured in the glass tube in which ballpoint pen refills are supplied, glued to the vine.

31a, 31b   A modern design. A major rhythm of curves created by aspidistra accompanied by a minor rhythm of diagonals, cut iris. Notice how important the diagonals are to the design. Compare **a** with **b** where the two rudbeckia contribute very little to a design that is lacking the visual depth and weight of the diagonals.

32a Greater freedom of design is expressed by *not* placing a strong accent on a central axis. The eye stops on the dahlia and movement elsewhere is checked. The vein of the lower *Verbascum* leaf leads to the dahlia, the enclosed central space adds further weight and the tallest stem presses it down on to the inharmonious base.

32b Reverse the stems and omit the dahlia allowing the weight of the partly enclosed spaces to operate, and the design gains movement and lightness.

33 The open form suggests protection, shelter, peace, embryo, depending on your viewpoint. Created with palm spathes and roses it is a modern design of great simplicity. The container is covered by fungus mounted in Polyfilla which also adds textural interest.

34 After clipping the camrose palm to shape for the design shown on plate **17**, I have threaded the remains together and reshaped a 'leaf'. These are used here for the interpretive abstract, 'Eden'. (The covering for the wood holder is made by putting a well-pinholder on to a plate and piling Polyfilla round it, shaping and scoring it. When nearly dry the well-pinholder is removed and when dry the Polyfilla can be coloured to suit.)

35 A modern design to suggest 'Lightning' using tortured willow to contrast with the severe vertical placing of the narcissi. Care has been taken to prune the willow so that the design has unity through repetition.

36 This design relies entirely for its effect on the shape of the lily stem. Slightly swollen in the centre and most interestingly curved, it needed only the very light *Alstromeria* placed to repeat the diagonal movement and the rolled aspidistra to make a transition to the container, allowing the container to act as a contrasting movement.

37 A modern design. Enclosed space makes a strong element in any design. In this design the visual weight of the small enclosed areas at the top is counteracted by the larger space below framed by the one pink carnation. This also makes a strong centre of interest. Texturally related, the seaweed root on the left makes a secondary centre of interest balancing the curling stem on the lower right. The *Hosta aurea* leaf relates in shape to the container and the upper enclosed space, and contrasts in colour with the carnation.

38 A modern design. A design relying entirely on the space areas. The fresh wistaria tendrils are given interest and colour by jasmine and polyanthus in the shell.

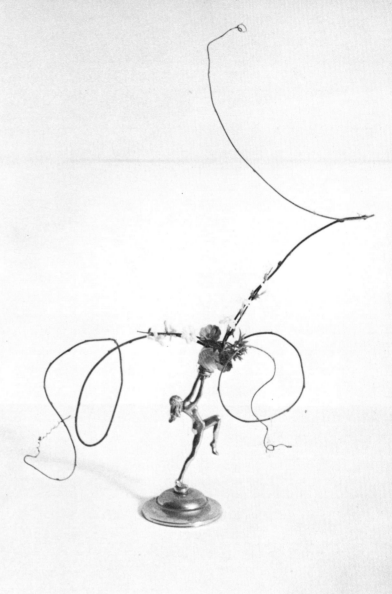

39 A modern design. A squash bottle, extended with the cardboard centre of a toilet roll, covered with Polyfilla and painted, makes an interesting container for this design, which relies on the vine for its interest. Particularly significant to the balance is the shadow enclosure at the bottom of the design. Cover with your finger to see the difference.

40 A modern design, based on triangles, which derives considerable strength from the repetition of the parallel diagonal lines on the left. Additional emphasis is created by the contrasting downward diagonal on the right, which is also the key unit to make a line of continuance through the design.

41 The related lines of pine branches make a dancing movement in this modern arrangement, enhanced by the placement of the begonia leaves. The eye runs round the outline of the leaves. Because they are overlapped the eye is pushed back into the design giving a great sense of depth. The sense of depth is further emphasized by the textured markings on the pottery wing base.

42 A modern design, 'Room at the Top', to suggest the tensions of living in the modern high-rise apartment blocks. The dry 'flowers' are sections of iris seed-pod glued into a fir-cone. The zigzag of the diagonal creates the restless tension. The circle in this line relates to the hole in the container and to the *Allium*. The pottery container is by Joyce Withey.

43 'Lakeside'—a modern design using a home-made pottery container (suggesting the ripples on water), black painted twigs and marsh marigolds. Figurines are not used in modern and abstract design. This piece of embryo palm looked so like a duck, it was the inspiration of the design. To give perspective it is set on a home-made wing-shaped pottery base, indented with scissor jabs to give texture.

44 A semi-abstract design. As soon as lines cross, tension is created. In this design one bulrush thrusts up into space and gives the remainder of the design movement. The shorter narcissus is set at a diagonal *within* space and becomes very important. The enclosed areas created by the bulrush leaves (right) give interest and balance to the whole design.

45 Some material is very difficult to use decoratively. Here the aconda spathes have been emphasized by the aspidistra leaves and the design is given significance by throwing its shadow on to the background. The smaller enclosed spaces on the left balance the larger spaces on the right. In this case, the aspidistra leaf on the left is most important for balance and emphasis. Try covering it to see why.

46 The bold forms of twisted aspidistra leaves give movement to this design. They frame the minor centre of interest in the marguerite. Strong bottom interest and movement is created by the white marguerite drawing the eye out and the dark rosette of euphorbia leaves pulling the eye in.

47 Short diagonals of iris leaves create additional depth and movement. They also make a stronger design by contrasting with the curve of the tallest aspidistra, greatly increasing its significance.

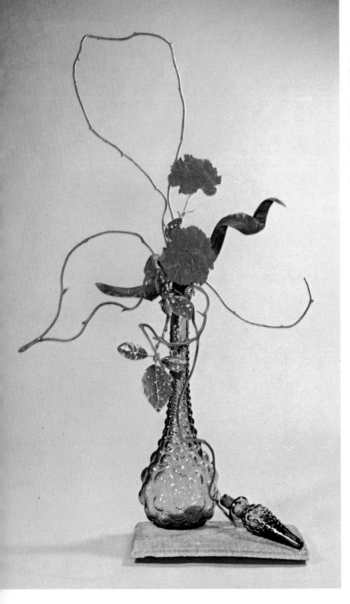

48 In this modern arrangement, a glass bottle supports Russian vine stems looped into planes or implied planes. The curled poinciana seed-pods contrast with the vine and emphasize the implied plane, right. Trimmed variegated aucuba relates to the container in colour and to the cane loops (planes) in shape.

49 *Alstromeria* seed-heads frame the parsnip seed-head, with further emphasis from the ornopordon leaves making almost an *Art Nouveau* design! Note how extremely important the shape of space is to this design.

50 In this modern design the long strap-like leaves of palm have been curled on to themselves and stapled together and then mounted on a small piece of soft wood for easy insertion on to a pinholder. The three bulrushes run parallel to one edge of the triangular container and the iris, creating a contrasting pull to the diagonals of the bulrushes, are placed parallel to the other side of the container. This ensures a three-dimensional design viewable from any angle. The pinholder is covered with Polymer chips. These have been shaken on to a plate, sprayed with PVA glue, making a flexible 'mat' that can be broken and placed over the pinholder as desired.

51 Creating a most exciting swirling rhythm that seems to move differently as you look at it, two pieces of cane are given life by the placing of the peony and alchemilla leaf and by the irregular movement of the base.

52 Overlapping planes take the eye back into space and create depth. The material used is aspidistra leaves, cut fans of iris, asters and curled silver birch bark.

53 A modern design. A suggestion of transparency—we can see through one plane to view the one behind, thus creating great visual depth.

54 A modern design. Light shadow and converging lines suggest spatial movements that give depth to a design. The downward space created by the iris leaves is balanced by the sub-dominant begenia leaf—the solid balancing the void.

55 A modern design. The very large leaf of the shrubby clematis, cut short, balances the long length of the parsnip seed-head. Additional tensions between the dark green leaf and light pink asters give interest and vitality to this simple design.

56 A modern design. A Joyce Withey container with strong textural interest is emphasized with dried staghorn moss mounted on stripped ivy. The roses contrast in texture but relate in shape, balance and interest being created by the spaces made by the curving iris leaf (steamed into shape).

57 Eucalyptus bark and roses make this delightful modern design which relies heavily on texture, space tensions and the varied values of light and shade for its effect.

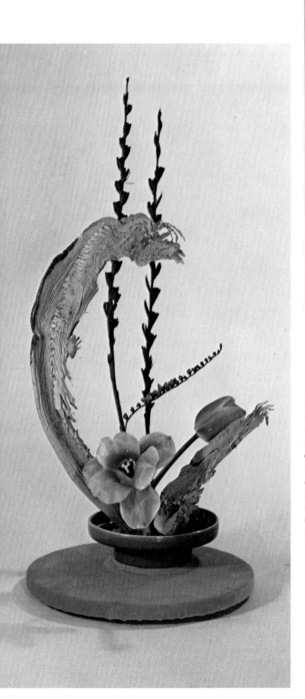

58 Non-objective, decorative abstract. This strong diagonal design is set in a bark container, the two silvery contrasting diagonals are opened stems of *Kniphofia*. The geraniums are supported in Oasis, wrapped in plastic and secured in strips of bark to the Russian vine stems. A lichen-covered twig is used to cover the pinholder and at the same time draw the eye to the container. When using a diagonal in this way there is always a danger of pulling the design apart. This is why we have a repetition of line through the wood at the base of the geraniums on the left, the two white pithy stems and the lichen twig.

59 A modern design using embryo palm and seed-heads. Notice that one tulip is parallel to the palm, lower right, and a *Curtonus* seed-head is parallel to the tulip. This repetition is essential to give the necessary rhythm to this design.

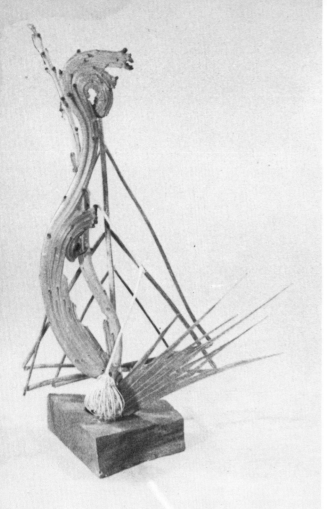

60 Intended by me to be an expressive abstract entitled 'The Musician'. My family's comments are unprintable! The inspiration was the faciated ash, the contrasts bent stems of cow parsley and a section of palm leaf.

61 Light is the main factor in the effect texture creates. A design based on a semi-ellipse. *Veratrum* leaves are deeply veined. By a low angle light this is emphasized. The hydrangea head also appears rough.

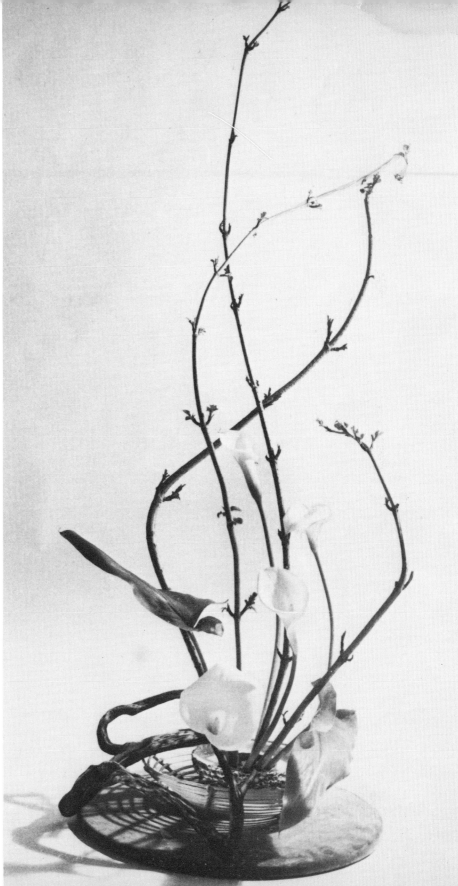

62 A strong rhythmic movement induced by the curved elderberry branches and the burnt gorse branch at the base. The lilies are placed to emphasize the same rhythm. The lower arum leaf is used to pull the eye back into the design and the upper leaf, used as a diagonal, emphasizes the upward movement of the branches. Try covering it with your finger to see how important it is.

63 An abstract design of great vigour made with manipulated cane and looped glycerined *Curtonus* leaves for contrast. The container is a rolled gramophone record. The geranium blooms are secured in the tops of black felt tip pens, fastened to the cane. To shape the cane it has been soaked, wound overall with thin galvanized wire and bent to the desired shape. Once dry the wire is removed. It was subsequently sprayed matt black.

64 Emphasis on form. Aspidistra leaves manipulated into curves in the steam from a kettle spout are glued to a central spine of bulrushes. A change in texture is given by the use of curved palm spathes and mounted curled silver birch bark.

65 An endeavour to suggest a quiet day in spring. Severely pruned branches supported in a well-pinholder with young leaves of begonia set to give a slow spiralling rhythm. The container is polystyrene packing from a camera, with a different polystyrene box used above and below—the whole painted soft blue, but giving the appearance of carved stone.

66 An abstract design, 'Passiontide', intended to suggest that the Crucifixion leads into Resurrection. Even untitled this makes a strong design.

67 A modern design. It is quite permissible to cut and reshape material. Here the whole of one side of each branch has been stripped to allow interest of the remainder to function as part of the design. A related ellipse is made by the palm husks. The *Hosta* leaves relate to the circular 'pewter' plate, to the ellipse of the other materials and add a stepped horizontal emphasis. The two brilliant red ginger torch lilies, set forward and backward, give depth and dominance.

68 A container made for me by Joyce Withey creates a dramatic interest before one starts to design. To find blackened gorse and prune it to just the right shape to complete this design took a long time. Nothing but a *Lilium auratum* could make the contrast that is so vital.

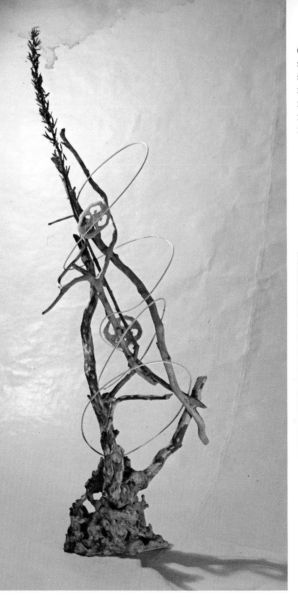

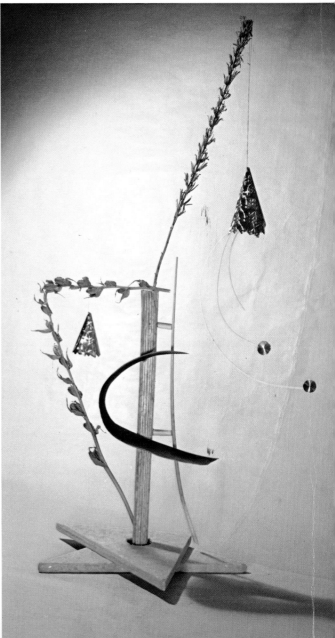

69 A stabile—absolutely stationary, static, stable. The swirling cane suggests movement but nothing actually moves. The sections of loofa relate to the design and make interesting eye pauses.

70 A stamobile—part static and part mobile. The curved bark has been darkened to emphasize contrast and to repeat the curves in the canes of the mobile. Special silver foil introduces a 'sparkling' interest as the mobiles constantly move, changing the design.

71 This particular arrangement gave me a lot of problems! The container is a plastic bleach bottle with the top removed. On to this has been stuck, at irregular angles, slivers of polystyrene. It was painted with emulsion and then sprayed lightly matt black. To accentuate this I chose the vertical seed-stems of mullein. To contrast in texture and yet relate in form I chose the tiger lilies, leaving the leaves and buds on their stems. Finally they had to be seen in a large spatial frame if they were to look anything. The answer was the wide sweeping arc of dried pine with the little stubbly bits still attached. It relates in texture to the container. The cones are most important to make it contribute its effect to the total design. The light fungus swings the eye into the design and adds a subordinate emphasis. Try covering various parts of the design and considering the effect produced.

72 A modern design. Pussy willow has often been used for curved material. Here, taken a stage further, the large spaces delineated by the willow are balanced by the leaves and red tulips. At the same time the eye is led down through the willow to the horizontals of the fungi and thence by repetition to the bases.

73 A modern design. Three dried *Ligularia* leaves are the dominant placements, making a strong rhythm by repetition. They relate to the loops of *Curtonus* leaves and the heavier twisted gorse branch. To add interest five flocked polystyrene balls, mounted on a loop of cane, give movement and lightness to the design, being a little darker than the fungus but the same velvety texture as the seed-pods curving at the base. There is a proportion of dark, medium and light values here that is very satisfying.

74a, 74b To make abstract design interpretive depends not only on the selection of material but also on its placement. Compare these two designs, using very similar material: an odd shaped piece of wood, a loop of cane, *Hosta*, hellebore and aspidistra leaves. Both suggest tension but of different sorts: **a** by placing the lily high and keeping the aspidistra high it suggests surprise, even fear; **b** by softening the curve of the cane, extending the weight of the aspidistra with an additional dried leaf and removing the lily, the nature of the tension has changed to attack.

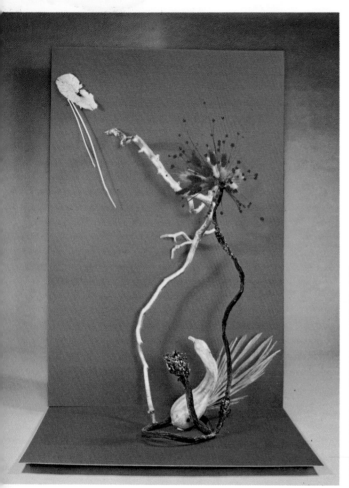

75a Backgrounds for abstract arrangements can make a tremendous difference to the whole design. On the left is a design to suggest 'space probe'.

75b On the right a piece of brown chiffon has been lightly sprayed with silver paint over the silhouette of a maple leaf. The 'cloud effect' over the same background entirely alters the effect. Perhaps it should now be called 'Orbit'! The black material is seaweed, which can be soaked and shaped as desired, the oblique green is montbretia leaves stapled together, fanned out and dried in silica gel.

76a Backgrounds can be devised in many ways. Their major use would be in show or exhibition work, when they become an integral part of the design. This is made from scrim, painted with an abstract design in bleach. The abstract design in front uses glycerined *Curtonus* leaves, cut and fanned at intervals. Hogweed supports the chrysanthemums in water-retaining material and dried aspidistra are used to contribute curves. Considerable care is taken over the space intervals, the light/dark relationships and the tensions. Notice too that the upright *Curtonus* is set just off the vertical to avoid a static balance.

76b A Joyce Withey container has been introduced, on its end, the curved edge giving an immediate strong contrast, so that the design has been altered with an emphasis on the diagonals and related circles between the container and the opuntia stem circles. Consequently the whole design has more vitality.

77 A modern arrangement. Looped and stapled together these palm leaves emphasize the circular movements within the container. The contrasting movement of the branch makes a dominant sweep and could lead the eye out of the design except that the hole in the container pulls it back. This relates to the movement on the container, thence to the gourd and back into the circles of palm.

78 Composite bases, overlapped and contributing a design element in themselves, are emphasized by the balotta and sisyrinchium, both of which repeat the horizontal movement as also does the vertical seed-pod *Delonix regia*. Contrasts of horizontal and vertical elements placed apart will always create a sense of depth, but cause the vertical to predominate.

79 Tension, suspense, movement are all incorporated in this design—a decorative abstract, with careful consideration given to repetition of shapes, values and space intervals but, because of the strong diagonal emphasis, a design that almost moves as you look at it.

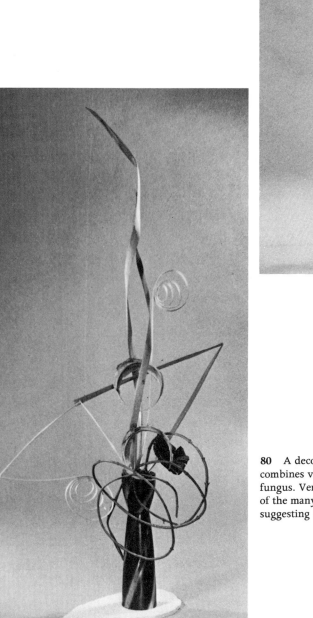

80 A decorative abstract that combines vine, iris leaves and fungus. Very light yet, because of the many enclosed spaces, suggesting considerable bulk.

81 'The Dance'—the background here is intended to suggest stage lights and has been made by sticking coloured card on to a background and base board. The branch has been painted with tempera paint to highlight the effect. The green flower is in fact a dried hellebore seed-head.

82 This design can be seen against a plain background in black and white. Here it was intended to make it interpretive by linking it to the background. PVA glue has been trailed on the background paper, and when dry it has been wiped over with swabs of coloured inks to suggest the troubles in Ireland. Nothing extra has been done to the design in front and yet the effect is totally different. This background method lends itself to a vast number of variations.

83 'Homeward Bound'—an abstract arrangement intended to suggest the roadside scenery as one flashes past! In fact the curves have been carefully manipulated to suggest a feeling of progressive distance. The hydrangeas are placed to carry the eye into the design and to contrast in texture and form. The fresh cupressus has been drastically clipped and the denuded twigs wired into position and allowed to dry before removing the wire. The lower branch is secured by the method shown in the section on 'Mechanics'.

84 Polystyrene can be cut to any shape. In this case it has been cut and mounted on the outside of a cylindrical container. Two well-pinholders are used. The pussy willow was wired into position whilst still young and left to dry this way. One or other peony would have been better omitted as two tend to pull the design apart. This container was later made in pottery for me by Joyce Withey.

85 Curved, trimmed beech, to give a wind-blown effect, is mounted in a base of Polyfilla. A well-pinholder set into the plaster whilst wet and removed before drying is complete, makes the branch stand firmly and enables tulips and *Mahonia* (or anything else) to be arranged at will. When dry the Polyfilla is rubbed over with brown and black shoe polish and is almost indistinguishable from natural bark. This stands on a slate base. The design is more free-form than modern but illustrates an important technique with the wood.

86 Just to remind ourselves what the traditional style embraces. This all-foliage arrangement in the form of a triangle is mainly interesting because of its textural changes making a design within a design, and creating a line of continuance. It has symmetrical balance, transitional material and radial design.

87 A rotten stump, with all
the decayed wood removed,
treated with preservative and
sprayed with varnish, can make
a delightful sculpture in its own
right. (Photograph by T. Elves)

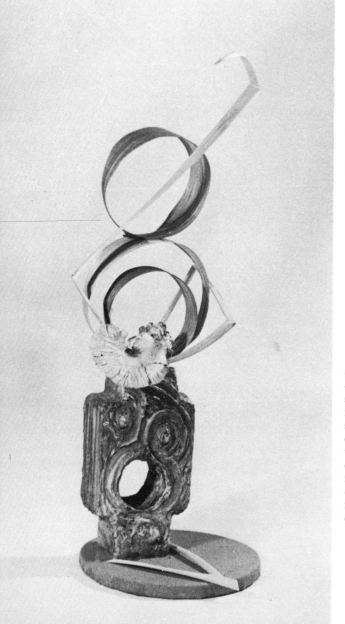

88 An abstract arrangement. This is a home-made
container, made from cardboard covered in Polyfilla. The two
sides are first shaped, then a strip about 5 cm (2 in) wide
inserted between them and glued into position, including a
strip round the hole. (A candle cup pinholder fits into the top
of the container.) It is painted brown and sprayed with
varnish. Curled *Curtonus* leaves, Sellotaped together,
emphasize the circular movements within the container, the
fungus further emphasizes this, the small dark centre
drawing the eye into the design. Dried iris leaves have been
folded to make a contrasting movement, including one piece
on the base.

89 A very similar design to **41** but staged in a window so that the sun could add shadows for effect. Lighting is always important and some future research will no doubt produce controlled methods open to all for show work.

90 'Alert'—an abstract design featuring a piece of burnt wood on a slate base. A teasel relates in texture to the burnt wood and in shape to the hole within it. The curve of the palm spathe contrasts in texture but relates to the curve within the burnt wood. The *Hemerocallis* contrast in texture to the wood, but relate in colour to the palm spathe and dried *Kniphofia*. The *Kniphofia* give depth to the design and make a contrasting movement to the burnt wood. The day lilies are each wired into position, their stem ends in Oasis in plastic. In fact, because they only last one day anyway, they can be used with or without water.